REDEMPTION

REDEMPTION

A Rebellious Spirit, a Praying Mother, and
the Unlikely Path to Olympic Gold

Bryan Clay

with Joel Kilpatrick

THOMAS NELSON
Since 1798

NASHVILLE   DALLAS   MEXICO CITY   RIO DE JANEIRO

© 2012 Bryan Clay

All rights reserved. No portion of this book may be reproduced, stored in a retrieval system, or transmitted in any form or by any means—electronic, mechanical, photocopy, recording, scanning, or other—except for brief quotations in critical reviews or articles, without the prior written permission of the publisher.

Published in Nashville, Tennessee, by Thomas Nelson. Thomas Nelson is a registered trademark of Thomas Nelson, Inc.

Unless otherwise noted, Scripture quotations are taken from the Holy Bible, New Living Translation. © 1996, 2004, 2007. Used by permission of Tyndale House Publishers, Inc., Wheaton, Illinois 60189. All rights reserved.

Scripture quotations marked NKJV are from the New King James Version®. © 1982 by Thomas Nelson, Inc. Used by permission. All rights reserved.

ISBN 978-1-62090-055-0

Printed in the United States of America

CONTENTS

INTRODUCTION

Every second, every centimeter counts in the decathlon. Blow an event once, and you just might hand your next-closest competitor a ticket to the Olympic Games.

It was forty-one days before the 2008 Olympics in Beijing, China, and it seemed as if I was about to give away my only chance to get there. I had come into the Olympic Trials in Eugene, Oregon, a heavy favorite. But my performance so far was more Junior Olympics than Olympic gold medalist. One more mistake and I might as well count myself out of the Beijing Olympics altogether—missing the dream I had pursued most of my adult life.

Not another 1992, I kept thinking. *Please, God, don't let this be another 1992.*

The famous Dan and Dave decathlon debacle occurred during the 1992 Trials. Dan O'Brien, a favorite to medal, had failed to get a score in the pole vault. He was the best decathlete at that time, and he'd had a good meet going until the pole vault. Then that one bad event at Trials caused his 1992 Olympic hopes to vanish. This came after a huge public relations campaign by Reebok, which broadcast Dan and Dave (Johnson) commercials all over television to elevate the competition between the two premier athletes leading up to the games. Even more painful was that just a few weeks after losing at the Trials, Dan set a world record for points in a decathlon in France. His 8,891 points beat the Olympic gold medalist Robert Zmelik by 547 points.

Any athlete knows this hard fact about the Trials: it's all or nothing. U.S. track and field athletes have to place in the top three *and* meet the Olympic standards to go to the Olympics. Miss one or the other, and you won't go. Have an off day in just one event, and you probably won't go. That is why the U.S. Olympic team is widely considered the toughest team in the world to make. There are only three openings in each event, and athletes are not chosen by a prior ranking system. It doesn't matter how well you performed the previous month, the previous year, or over the course of your lifetime. You have to show up on that day and be the best. Period.

Now I might be humbled the same way that Dan O'Brien had been.

My performance was far from what I had expected. I had gotten to Eugene a week early to practice, and everything had gone well. Better than well. I had landed a massive jump during practice, flying 7.70 meters (25 feet 3 inches) from a short approach, meaning I had taken half the number of steps I usually take. That is huge for a decathlete. I felt great mentally, physically, emotionally, and spiritually. All the commentators, coaches, and athletes expected me to crush the field. And to be honest, that was weighing on me. I wanted to live up to their expectations. I wanted to make the team again, as I had in 2004. I had narrowly missed a gold then in what was the most competitive and high-scoring decathlon in the modern history of the games. Now I was hungry to nab the gold.

But by the time the Trials started, my great practices were a memory.

The long jump was a nightmare. The 25 feet I had jumped in practice seemed as if it had never happened. My body didn't soar or fly; it thudded—7 meters 39 centimeters, a full 15.5 inches shorter than what I had hoped for. I stepped out of the sand pit with a terrible feeling in my stomach, knowing that I had just made it even more difficult for myself to win. Other guys were having really good meets, walking around the practice area smiling, heads up, confidently preparing for the next events. Thoughts that I was already vanquished kept shooting through my brain and making it harder for me to concentrate on what I needed to do.

In the decathlon you try to build up points in your strongest events. Doing just so-so in your best events forces you to have to make up those points elsewhere, which could be impossible since you are already performing at your peak ability. And trying too hard in other events pulls you out of your rhythm. Instead of relaxing, you force it and make more mistakes. For reasons I could not fathom, my peak that day seemed lower than normal. It didn't matter that I had gotten positive press coverage or that some competitors were considered long shots. What mattered was who showed up on that day and put together the best score in ten events. So far the competition was winning.

In the past I had always been very good at compartmentalizing each result in my mind, building a wall between the past and the present. My iron rule of competition had always been to put each event behind me and move on to the next one, no matter how well or poorly I did. No athlete can afford to let the elation of a good performance or the pain of a bad one affect his or her next event. Success or failure can throw you off your rhythm and take you out of your zone. But this time the wall kept crumbling and disappointments kept flooding in. I was unable to escape the bitter memories of my substandard performance. I dragged those thoughts with me to the next warm-up area like so much dead weight.

This state of mind certainly did not help my shot put performance. The shot seemed heavier, my movements and steps tighter and less fluid. I had a bad throw. Now it wasn't just a fluke, it was a trend: Bryan Clay, gold medal favorite in Beijing, was in danger of not even making the team.

I groaned inwardly as I left the shot put area. *This is not how it's supposed to happen*, I thought. *If I don't pull this together, I'll be watching the games from my couch. Everything I've worked for these eight years will be lost—all the expectations, all the hopes that my family and I have had. The thousands of hours of practice—it could all just disappear.*

> The long jump was a nightmare. . . . My body didn't soar or fly; it thudded.

Feeling defeated, I went into the high jump area and had a really bad warm-up, which is unusual for me. I could tell that I had lost the mental game. I had to get away from the competition for a moment, so I walked off the track and headed for the bathroom under the bleachers. Hanging my head and slumping my shoulders, I couldn't even fake happiness for the cameras. As I was walking, I heard one of my coaches yell down to me from the stands: "Bryan, stop messing around! We just need to get third."

Third! Who was talking about third? We had never considered getting third. I was supposed to win the meet and then win Olympic gold. That was the script we were using. For a moment it seemed that someone had taken away that script in the middle of my performance and replaced it with a new one I had never seen before. I didn't know what to do.

I realized that my coaches were panicking. They could see in my posture that I was disappointed in myself; they knew the poison of defeat was threatening to seep into my remaining performances.

But still the phrase rang in my ear: "We just need to get third."

My mind swirling, my heart aching, I retreated under the bleachers and did the only thing I knew to do at a time of crisis: I began praying.

"God, You need to come down here and get this thing figured out," I said, fuming. "This is not how it's supposed to happen." I have to admit, it was not a very gracious prayer.

I was exasperated and angry. I felt I had been led into a situation where I would now humiliate myself in front of everyone—sports fans, my family, my coaches, and my fellow athletes. If this was God's plan for my life, I did not want any part of it. And I told Him so.

"I don't want to do this meet if this is how it's going to be," I said, and the thought of not finishing the meet seemed momentarily attractive. Maybe some little injury would occur, and I could have an excuse to withdraw—an absolutely insane thought, given how much of my life I had devoted to achieving this goal. Yes, I believed athletics was my God-given gift and my calling, but now I felt so beleaguered that I was beginning to question whether or not *that* was true and whether the pressure was even worth it. Would the goal I had pursued for most of my life justify all the effort I had put in? I wasn't sure anymore.

> The poison of defeat was threatening to seep into my remaining performances.

My prayers elicited no answer from God until about thirty seconds later when I was walking back to the track. That was when I heard Him say clearly and firmly to my heart: *Bryan, I do not expect you to be perfect. I just expect you to do your best. I'll make it good enough.*

The words hit me hard, and I stopped walking. Their effect was profound on my mind, my body, my emotions, and my spirit. I stood there and replayed them in my mind: *I do not expect you to be perfect. I just expect you to do your best. I'll make it good enough.* For the first time that day, relief came over me like the cold, relieving rush of fluids from an IV. The tension of disappointment, the stress of high expectations, and the tightness in my body melted away. I felt free to do what I did best.

"Okay," I said in return, "I'm just going to do my best. I'll trust You to make it good enough. If I'm supposed to get third place or no place at all, fine."

With that new goal in mind I went back into the high jump warm-up area. My coaches stared hard at me, looking for clues in my demeanor. I think they liked what they saw. My head was up, I was walking with confidence, and my shoulders were squared again. I felt absorbed in the next task. The past had disappeared behind one of those walls, and I didn't care about what I had done in the other events. As far as I was concerned, I was starting over. I got into my rhythm for the high jump.

Suddenly I was having fun again.

I started my run, gained speed, kept my eyes fixed on the bar, took that last step, and launched myself into the air. As I arched my back and soared upward, I could only wonder: *Will it be enough?*

His Plan, His Purpose

Many athletes say their rise to the top was unlikely, and that may be true. But I think I am one of the most unlikely Olympic decathletes in the history of the games. I am just five feet ten inches tall in a sport where the average height is well above six feet. I am not as big as the typical decathlete, just 178 pounds versus 195 or more. I am the smallest decathlete to ever win an Olympic gold medal. I do not have long arms or legs, which help when thrusting a sixteen-pound steel ball as far as you can or hurling a discus. I'm a pretty fast runner, and that has helped me, though my weakest event is the 1500 meters (almost a mile)—one that I've had to accommodate my entire career by scoring high in other events.

My background gave me no hope of being a professional athlete. There were no sports stars in our family, no great lineage to carry on—no one in my family was active at all in sports. I didn't even come from an intact home; my parents' divorce tore me up and, in my younger years, put me on a path toward almost certain criminality. The odds were in favor of my landing in jail, getting hooked on drugs, or being involved in a teenage pregnancy—not in favor of competing at any level in anything.

I also got a late start in the decathlon. By the time I went to college on a sports scholarship, I had participated in just two. Yet just a few years later, I was representing our country at the Olympics in Athens.

Perhaps the reason I became a two-time Olympic medalist was because what my mom said was true: God had a plan for me, and He was not going to let me screw it up.

He had a plan for me when I was beating up other kids and getting kicked out of schools in Hawaii.

He had a plan when I was partying and going to school drunk from the seventh grade on.

He had a plan when I was damaging my body on purpose and taking the first small steps toward suicide.

He had a plan when I believed that dreams never came true because, in my life, they never did.

He had a plan when, almost by chance, I joined a track team because the counselor told my mom that sports was the only thing that would keep me out of prison or the morgue.

He had a plan that would turn me, a flat-out bad kid with no future, into a world-class athlete and, more important, a loving husband and father.

God had a plan for me, and that is the only reason you are holding this book and the reason that two of the most coveted medals in all of sports are sitting in a drawer in my closet right now.

Along the way, God helped me discover the principles of success. Only when I began putting God first and putting these principles to work in my life did I find myself catapulted into the ranks of elite athletes. Before then, my life was in disarray. But when I chose to follow Christ wholeheartedly, I began to compete at a level I truly did not believe was possible for me.

> He had a plan that would turn me, a flat-out bad kid with no future, into a world-class athlete and, more important, a loving husband and father.

Learning to embrace God's way wasn't easy, but doing so made a world of difference. If I had not paid attention to Him and His way, someone else would have the Olympic medals. Someone else would be writing this book, perhaps not giving honor to God and not using the platform to talk about the importance of fatherhood in children's lives. And I wouldn't want that to happen.

I do not believe I was destined to be a decathlete. I do not believe I am extraordinarily gifted in any way. Like anyone else, I have natural talents, but they are not so great as to make anything certain. People tend to elevate Olympians and other athletes to a godlike level, as if we are born with a special gene that makes us outperform everyone else. But as someone who has spent his life in that community, I can tell you that is not true.

What separates elite athletes from everyone else has more to do with the choices they make along the way rather than their DNA. Those winning choices will become clear as I tell you my story. You will see just how unlikely my Olympic career has been and how I went from being a punk kid with little social value to being an athlete who loves God and his family and has a heart for people everywhere, especially kids from broken homes.

It is a story that God has told through the events of my life. And it is pretty amazing.

ONE
A DREAM BEGINS

When my mom was pregnant with me, she would hop the fence at a local university in Austin and walk the track, praying for the baby in her womb. She wasn't a believer in any particular religion at the time, but as she circled the rubberized track, gazing at the infield where the track and field events took place and looking up at the empty stands where people would gather for sporting events, she asked God to keep me safe, make me healthy, and give me purpose in my life. Though her spiritual beliefs were murky, when it came to the most important thing in her life—me at the time—she turned instinctively to God. I have always wondered whether God heard those prayers offered up from that 400-meter oval and answered my mom by making her first child a track and field athlete.

My dad enlisted in the military soon after my birth, and we were transferred to San Francisco in 1983. The move must have provided some personal relief to my Japanese mother and African American father. Their interracial marriage had been subject to some discrimination in Texas. We moved onto the army base at the Presidio with a view of the Golden Gate Bridge from our house. Our home, which was light and airy, backed up to the hills. Every morning I woke up and saw a mountain lion perched at the top of a hill. Deer walked into our yard, squirrels and raccoons came to the back door, and we threw bread to them. A bobcat roamed the neighborhood, too, and a skunk stole food from people's trash cans. I was young and life was full of magic.

My dad worked in the military prison, and one of my earliest memories is walking through the jail with him one day. Dad explained that those men sitting in their cells were good people who had made bad decisions and were suffering the consequences. The scene did not make a big impact on me then, but later, during my brushes with the law, I thought back to those guys, stripped of their dignity and their freedom. At times it seemed that this had been the true vision of my future—an alternate and more powerful vision from the one my mom had earnestly prayed for during her pregnancy. It was a repudiation of her hopes and dreams and mine. Soon I would sense these competing visions for my life and feel the strong tension between destruction and destiny.

My dad was a strong and welcome presence in the household, and unlike other members of the military, he never had to go on extended tours of duty away from home. I was with him every day. As you would expect of a man in his position, he was physically fit, and he picked me up and played rough-and-tumble with me, the way dads do. We talked about the animals I saw in the neighborhood.

I loved seeing my dad and my mom together. She was slender, with long black hair parted in the middle and hanging down to the middle of her back. I thought she was the prettiest woman I had ever seen. When my brother, Nikolas, was born in San Francisco four years after I was born, he came into a happy family. Those good times, however, were all too brief.

Witnessing Excellence

After my dad got out of the military, we moved to Hawaii, where my mom had grown up and where her family still lived. My mom's large extended family suddenly became the dominant presence in our lives. My mom was born in Japan, where my grandfather was in military intelligence for the U.S. during World War II. I had seen him and my grandmother only once when they visited us in San Francisco. We called him Jiji, a derivative of the Japanese word for grandfather— *ojiichan*, which was hard for us to say. My grandmother was known to us as Baba, short for *obaachan*, which is Japanese for grandmother.

Jiji was like a traditional samurai: strict, strong-willed, knowing right from wrong and not letting anyone tell him otherwise. To this day I regard him as something like the shogun, or leader, of our family. He was loud and forceful and had no problem yelling at people to get his point across. Yet I knew that he loved my brother and me, and he was generous to us, buying us toys or clothes or whatever we needed for school. He owned a successful small business and several rental houses, and I had the feeling that in everything he did, he was fighting for his life. He was not afraid to work hard to provide for his family. He drove a Cadillac and kept everything he owned in perfect working order. The lessons I learned from him played a major part in my becoming a champion.

My family lived in Palolo Valley on what Hawaiians call the "town side," or the Honolulu side, of the island, where my grandfather owned three houses on one lot. Two of them were rented out to nonfamily members, and we moved into the house in the middle. The view from the house was of a verdant hillside that ascended to the central mountain range on the island. We caught the bus for a quarter and went to the beach, where we swam and played.

Our weekly routine, though, was mostly dictated by the family business. My grandparents' company, Kewalo Pickle, sold foods prepared according to Baba's original recipe. They pickled kimchi, a type of Korean spicy cabbage, as well as cucumbers and daikon, which is like a big, white, ugly radish. They did it all in a shop housed in a former train warehouse in Honolulu's Chinatown. My grandparents lived in a condo not far from the shop. My dad worked for my grandfather, so we went to the shop very early every morning. My brother and I slept in the back of the car on the way there. We ate breakfast at the shop and then went to school. More often than not, we came back to the shop after school and spent most of our weekends there too. My mom always had a secretarial job elsewhere in town.

> The lessons I learned from him played a major part in my becoming a champion.

Initially I had no responsibilities. I hung around the shop and played with my cousins. We were free to roam, more or less, supervised by many aunts and uncles who worked there. We even bathed in the big stainless steel vats on wheels because we were hardly ever home. But as we grew up, my grandfather taught us to work. Soon I was peeling daikon, loading the packing machine, measuring the food, cutting the hearts out of the cabbages, and sticking the various vegetables into the cleaning machine, the slicing machine, and the packing machine. The packing room was everybody's favorite because it was the only air-conditioned room in the building.

I became comfortable with the rhythms of the small processing plant, and I enjoyed the praise I got when I did a good job. I also liked using a knife to peel and cut the vegetables. To this day the feeling of grabbing a long white daikon off the conveyor belt, peeling it, and tossing it in a bin has stayed with me. Put a knife in my hand, set me in front of a conveyor belt, and I could do the same thing for hours on end, working to the rhythm of the machines in my memory.

The end results of all our labor were thousands of small clear packages of pickled foods bearing the Kewalo Pickle label—and our family's honor. Kewalo Pickle was Jiji's pride because everybody on the island knew it was his company. As I was able, I helped my uncles deliver the food to grocery stores all over the island, packing the boxes, replacing inventory, and making our packages look nice so people would buy them. As I got older, I became very aware that whatever I did, good or bad, reflected not just on me or my parents but on all of my family members and the business. Yet this knowledge rarely affected my behavior, especially when I reached adolescence and decided I was my own man.

I worked in the family business or with my relatives in other ways from the time I moved to Hawaii all the way through high school. My auntie would call and say, "Can Bryan Ezra come down and help out today at the shop?" Or my uncle would ask me to help him with deliveries. Or my grandmother would have me help her in the garden, pulling weeds, cutting grass, building greenhouses, and rearranging plants. If I wasn't working in the garden or the shop, my grandfather always had another job he wanted help with—building something my grandmother needed or repairing something at one of his rental houses. He taught me how to plumb, weld, use a grinder, handle a drill, and work with most tools. I was painting and roofing homes even when I was in grade school.

My mother and my aunts used to tell me, "One of these days you're going to really appreciate what your grandfather is teaching you." And I used to say, "Not a chance." The older I got, the more I hated the work, and I particularly hated being forced to work with Jiji on Saturdays when my cousins, who were all girls, often were allowed to go to the beach instead. Jiji woke me up at 7:00 a.m. to help him, and I'd be steaming because I knew that my cousins were cavorting in the ocean while I peeled daikon or fixed a leaky roof.

Of course, I couldn't have asked for a better education. I learned so many things from Jiji, and much of my mental toughness comes from the lessons he taught and the stories he told while we worked together. I saw in his example that things should be made perfect whenever possible.

Now, on the track, I work to be technically perfect. I do things again and again until I get them right. I expect myself to be able to visualize it and then do it. That's what my job is, and a lot of that expectation comes from Jiji, who was a perfectionist in his work. Because of him, I'm not afraid to get dirty or take on a job or a challenge. I was learning things that would help me become a successful husband, father, and athlete, even though I didn't understand that at the time. Without those early lessons I am reasonably certain I wouldn't have done nearly as well in any of those areas.

Downward Spiral

Home life became difficult as soon as we moved to Hawaii. My mom and dad seemed to be looking for answers, seeking happiness but not finding it. They started to fight a lot, and their fights became physical. Gone were the peaceful days of our San Francisco life. The predominant mood went from innocence and fun to anger and violence.

For one thing, my parents began smoking marijuana together. The presence of the drug brought sadness and more tension. At a young age I knew how to roll a joint, just from watching them. One evening they went to buy marijuana with my brother and me in the backseat. We drove slowly through a neighborhood that even I as a child knew was a bad place. My dad gave my mom some money and stopped the car. A man came up to the passenger window, my mom gave him the money, and he handed her a bag.

"Check it," Dad said. "Check it to make sure it's good."

Mom opened the bag, smelled it, and said, "It's fine." Then she put it in the glove compartment. We drove off, but before we had gone very far, my dad pulled over to check it. He discovered that it was fake or inferior.

"I told you to check it!" he said and then cursed at her. That started another one of the big fights that Nik and I had come to expect—and dread.

Life got worse, faster than I was able to handle it. When my parents fought, my brother and I learned to retreat to our bedroom and shut the door. I often held him while we heard dishes breaking against the wall in the kitchen, my parents screaming, doors slamming, and my mom crying. My brother was scared, and I tried to reassure him by saying, "It's going to be okay." But I had no confidence that things were going to be okay.

Nik and I almost never fought with each other. Our personalities were opposites. I was

Life got worse, faster than I was able to handle it.

confrontational and told people exactly how I felt. He was quieter and kept his feelings inside. I always felt the need to protect him because of his tender heart and younger age. We wouldn't come out of our room until the yelling stopped for good, which usually happened only when my dad decided to take a drive. We emerged carefully to see what damage had been done to the house.

On a couple of occasions my dad's anger turned on my brother.

Dad was still waking us up at 4:30 a.m. to go to my grandfather's shop, and Nik, who has never been a morning person, sometimes started crying. One time my dad whaled on him with a rolled-up newspaper to the point that Nik got a bloody nose. I felt helpless as Nik cried and cried.

Something had changed drastically in our family. The heaven of my earliest years had turned into a confusing hell from which I could see no escape.

Through it all, I felt that my dad and mom loved us, but their behavior toward each other made no sense to us. After a fight, my mom would pull us aside, hold us together in her arms, and say, "I'm sorry, boys. Mommy and Daddy still love each other. We're just having a hard time right now."

If they loved each other, why did they spew so much hatred at each other at times? Why did they try to hurt each other physically? Why didn't they sit on the couch and hold hands and have quiet evenings watching television, like other parents did? Dad still hugged us and messed around with us like dads do. He was still my hero because he was my father. But the atmosphere of stress and uncertainty in the home was simply horrible.

TWO
A CAULDRON OF BLACK EMOTIONS

As I grew angrier and more unsettled, I got in serious trouble at school by fighting and often actually hurting other kids. The problem began in kindergarten. Sometimes the fights had a reason, a cause, or a trigger, but other times they didn't. The trigger was in my heart, where anger reached a point that it had to be released.

I attended a kindergarten that was entirely indoors, and I played basketball in the gym at recess. I had played a lot of basketball at the shop with my uncles, who had put up a hoop, and I was used to being around older people who knew the rules of the game. But the kids at school had no idea it was a game with rules. I would be dribbling the ball, and one of them would take the ball, foul me, or not dribble. Infuriated, I would say, "You can't do that," but they didn't care. They were playing; I was competing.

I got so mad that I would tackle them and punch them hard with my fists because I felt they had wronged me and wronged the game. I didn't like people breaking the rules. After tackling them, I sometimes held them down on the ground and bit their cheeks hard enough to do damage. The school had no choice but to call my parents. Soon the administrators told my mom, "If there's one more incident, we're going to have to ask Bryan to leave for good."

That one more incident happened one day at recess when I tackled a boy for violating the rules of a playground game. I bit him, squeezed him, hit him, and generally worked him over until an adult pulled me off the boy and took me to the principal's office. I remember sitting there, just the principal and me looking at each other across her desk. Molten fury filled me, and I didn't know what to do except to release it in volcanic eruptions of violence.

> Sometimes the fights had a reason, a cause, or a trigger, but other times they didn't. The trigger was in my heart, where anger reached a point that it had to be released.

"I'm going to call your mom, and she's going to be really upset," the principal said as she picked up the phone and dialed my home number.

Watching her dial, I felt the magma of rage boil over. While the principal was talking with my mom, I used my fingernails to scratch down my face so hard that strips of skin peeled off in long, vertical lines.

The principal had been looking down at papers on her desk. She glanced up at me and stopped talking. She was so horrified that she might have even dropped the phone. I had expressed myself in the only way I knew how. What I did to my face matched my feelings inside. That was my last day at that school.

I finished the year at St. Mark's. I don't remember getting in trouble there, maybe because there was a large outdoor playground that offered a lot more room to run. I did better in school, and my mom told me she was so proud of me when I graduated kindergarten. The school had a ceremony with an open house, and I showed her all the things I had made. I remember the pride emanating from her as I received a little graduation certificate. She smiled down at me with one of those big, heartfelt smiles full of hope. Somehow the year had been salvaged, and we both breathed a sigh of relief.

The relief was short-lived, however. In first grade I attended a new school, and right away I got into a name-calling match with a fifth grader. I wasn't afraid of anyone. My older uncles had made me tough. This kid was teasing me, calling me a girl's name. So I responded by calling him a bad name.

A teacher nearby heard me and asked, "What did you say?"

I lied and told her I had said something else, but she didn't buy it, so I met the principal of that school in the first of our many private consultations.

If someone looked at me the wrong way, I wanted to fight with him. If someone said something the wrong way, I wanted to fight with him. In Hawaii, respect was very important. Even at a young age, kids would defend their honor, so fistfights were common anyway. But I somehow got into more fights than anyone else, and on top of that, I didn't pay much attention to my studies. My grades were terrible—a C+ was cause for my parents to celebrate.

Disrupting the lesson, talking, getting kicked out of class—all of that became common for me. Often at these times, I walked in a circle and punched the door as hard as I could on each circuit until someone sent me to the principal's office.

The more my parents fought with each other, the more my anger built and the more I got into trouble. Every situation in my life seemed to lead to anger. My grandfather became angry with me for not doing a job as well as he expected. My teachers were angry with me for disrupting class and fighting. My dad was angry with me for something. I became angry because I was in trouble. Life was negatively charged and heading toward a bad conclusion. My mom's heart was broken little by little by every fight I had and every failing grade I received, adding to her distress over her marriage and life in general. I didn't believe in myself, and in spite of my love for my parents and brother, I hated my life.

Then I discovered my gift.

Good—but Good Enough?

It was on the playground that I began to realize I had some athletic talent. I loved football, and we took our shoes off and played tackle football in the grass at every recess. I was always the team captain or the first person picked because I was one of the fastest boys. I wasn't the fastest student though. One girl beat me regularly in races and became my main competitor for a while. But I hated to lose, so I competed as hard as anyone.

I could also jump pretty well, which was evident in fifth grade when we boys tried to dunk a basketball on an eight-foot rim on the playground. We ran barefoot on the hot basketball court and tried to stuff the ball, and though I wasn't taller than the other kids, I was one of the few who could do it. After running so long on the hot asphalt, my feet blistered so much that the pads became one big blister. I had to go home, pop the blister, and tear off the skin. Then my feet were so tender that I couldn't even run on the grass the next day. Yet that did not stop me from doing it again.

The local Pop Warner football coaches tried to recruit me to play by saying, "You're fast, and you can jump. You should come out for the team." But Mom wouldn't let me, probably because she didn't want me to fight other players.

In 1988, I was watching the summer Olympics with my mom

and dad, and I saw Carl Lewis run the 100-meter dash. I turned to them and said, "I want to do that when I get older." It was an isolated comment that led nowhere then. Even though I was athletic and loved playing outdoors all day, I didn't realize that sports could be a path toward accomplishment and a better life. In my mind an athlete had to play baseball, football, or basketball. Those were the only sports I really knew about since they were the only ones shown regularly on TV. Because the guys playing these sports were all well over six feet, I knew I couldn't be one of them, so I wrote myself off as a competitor.

The idea of being successful, making tons of money, partying, and getting all the girls was appealing. Even at a young age I wanted that life. I wanted to do whatever I wanted without getting in trouble with anybody. And I wanted to play all day. I didn't have specific athletic heroes except for whoever was making the most money that week or dating the prettiest girl. I had no spiritual direction, no sense that life could be used for good. I just wanted to indulge.

Occasionally professional athletes came to our school and talked to us, trying to motivate us to do well in life. I remember they said things such as, "You can be anything you want and do anything you want if you just work hard and stay focused." One of them talked about writing his goals on a note card and taping it to his bathroom mirror so he saw it every morning and knew what he was working for.

I didn't believe that these motivational speeches applied to me. Being the kid I was—not the smartest in school, always in trouble, not involved in organized sports—I looked at them and said, "There's no way I can do what you do. You were born to play football. You're six foot five, weigh 315 pounds, and run a 4.30 seconds 40-yard dash. I'll never be that big or strong. And I'm not as smart as you. I'm not going to college. I was just born dumb."

Separation

One morning my mom and I were at the shop. I was getting ready to go to school when she called me over to her. She was sitting at the desk where the bookkeeping was done.

"Bryan," she said, "would you still love Mom if she wasn't here?"

The question didn't make any sense to me.

"Yeah," I said, thinking, *Of course I'd love you, wherever you were.*

"Give me a kiss and have a good day at school," she said.

I went to school as usual. But when I came home that afternoon, my mom was gone.

Dad got on the phone and called the police, called my grandparents, called everybody we knew, but nobody had seen her. He then left Nik and me with relatives and bolted out the door to drive around looking for my mom. My brother and I had no idea what was going on.

Sometime later—it might have been days or hours—I spoke to my mom on the telephone. "Mommy's going to be gone for a little while," she said. I still didn't know what had happened; I was too young to grasp any of it.

Some weeks later I talked to her again on the phone, and she said, "Mommy's coming home, and I've got a surprise for you."

Dad, Nik, and I went to the airport to pick her up, and we were excited to see her again. The surprise was a water rocket—when it was pumped up with water, it flew into the sky. I found out later that she had left my dad to be with an old boyfriend back in Texas. They had made a promise when they were young that if they were both single at a certain time, they would reunite. She had fled her miserable life for a new life with this old flame. But when she arrived in Texas, she discovered that he had become a Christian. He started taking her to church, and my mom became a born-again Christian.

When she returned to Hawaii, she was completely different—devoted to Jesus and determined to change everything in her life. She wanted her new beginning to be the whole family's new beginning. She wanted us all to go to church, read our Bibles, and pray. But these demands just caused more problems between her and my dad. He had grown up in a Christian home and had always told me, "I know what Christianity is all about, but I'm not willing to be one of those guys who calls himself a Christian but doesn't live a Christian life. I'm not going to go to church on Sundays and lie about the life I'm living. That's not what I'm about. When I'm ready to be a Christian, I will make that decision and change my life and do it wholeheartedly. But I'm not ready to do that right now."

We went to church as a family for a while, but then Dad stopped going with us. My mom kept taking my brother and me to a little Pentecostal congregation in Waikiki with an African American woman serving as pastor. To us, it was like walking into the crazy ward. People were shouting, fainting, and speaking in tongues. Nik and I had never seen anything like it, and we looked at each other and laughed. But we soon came to love the worship time because everybody would jump up and down, and we would too. What other church let you do that? The rest of it, especially the long sermons, bored us, and we often fell asleep in the pews.

> **She was completely different—devoted to Jesus and determined to change everything in her life.**

The spiritual divide in our home caused the fights to get worse and become more frequent. Added to them were allegations of infidelity, and my mom became suspicious of where my dad was and what he was doing. One day he would not answer his phone, and she finally said aloud, "I know where he is." She asked someone to watch us and went to find him. Supposedly she saw his car somewhere it should not have been. There was a huge blowup, and the next thing I knew they were getting a divorce.

I do not remember how I found out about their divorce or who told us. I was not sad or brokenhearted initially. My brother was too young to understand what was happening. One day, though, I had to go to court. I remember sitting in the lobby of the courthouse and knowing that I was to go into the courtroom shortly and choose between my parents. My mom had prepped me beforehand: "The judge is going to ask who you want to live with, and you tell him, 'Mom.'" Then my aunt (my mom's sister), who for some reason was there to testify for my dad, came up to me and told me the opposite: "When they ask you who you want to live with, tell them your dad." I guess my mom was something of an outsider with some of her relatives, and they had taken my dad's side.

How could I choose? Who would I choose? I was terrified. I did not want to have to choose between them. I could not imagine rejecting either one of them, and I couldn't understand why I had to. I thought about it long and hard, and in my ten-year-old mind, I concluded that I would choose my mom because I felt that Dad would understand. If I chose him, my mom would never be able to forgive me. It would be such a blow to her that she would never recover. I felt my mom needed me and my brother needed me. I could explain my decision to Dad later.

I think about that now and am amazed that I had to contemplate such things, let alone be asked to make that decision. As it turned out, I never had to go into the courtroom because the decision was made for me: we were staying with Mom. I asked Dad later why he had not fought for us. He said that he couldn't put us through that struggle, so he told Mom to go ahead and take us: we would be better off with her anyway.

After the divorce, life did not improve. The fights were over, but the emotional loss hit my brother and me. I missed my dad terribly. At some point my mom got a restraining order against him, and we were not allowed to see him at all. She remained at silent war with him. Later, after the order had been lifted, my dad was five minutes late to pick us up one weekend, so my mom wrote him a note, left it on the door, and took us away so he couldn't pick us up.

"See?" she told us. "If your dad really loved you, he would be on time."

Such comments were hard for me to forget. Looking back, I see that she was talking out of her pain. She barely knew how to cope without my dad around. She did not have her driver's license at the time, and she had no education or money. Dad was barely making enough to offer any child support. We ate dinner at my grandparents' house every night, along with all my aunts, uncles, and cousins. But we were also on food stamps for a while as she tried to get a job.

Anytime I got into another fight, she would say, "If you don't get a grip now, you're going to end up just like your dad." But I loved my dad, and he loved me, and because he wasn't there, I longed for him even more. I did not want her to diminish who he was. I know now that the parent who gets the kids after a divorce gets stuck with all the hard things: preparing the meals, getting the kids ready for school, taking them to the doctor, administering discipline, and teaching the lessons. It's no wonder the noncustodial parent looks like the better option.

Bus Stop Reunion

I had not seen my dad for weeks, due to the restraining order. So I was completely caught off guard when one day, while playing at recess, I saw him through the school-yard fence. He was sitting on a bus stop bench near the playground. The restraining order was still in effect, but he was apparently violating it to see me. Full of joy, I ran across the grass toward him.

My dad's here! My dad's here! I kept saying to myself as I ran. In those few seconds I thought that maybe he was going to take me away and everything was going to be better. Maybe I would have the life I dreamed about.

But he was not there to take me away. He just wanted to spend a few furtive moments with his son. We talked through the fence for a while, and he asked how everything was going with me and asked about Nik. He wouldn't let me get Nik because he was afraid he was too young to understand and would tell Mom. He also told me not to let Mom know I had seen him. Then the bell rang, and I was sad to have to go back to class.

"I miss you, Dad," I told him.

"I miss you, too, son," he said. "I love you guys so much. Everything's going to be okay."

We met like that several times, sitting on opposite sides of the fence during recess. After that, everywhere I went, I was looking for my dad. I wanted to see him, to be with him, to have the strength of a father in my life. I prayed for a long time that he and my mom would get back together, and for a while I thought they had broken up because of something I did. They had always fought when I got into trouble.

Those thoughts of Dad coming back into the family eventually gave way to daily realities. I was shouldering the task, with my mom, of caring for my brother. I had to walk him to kindergarten in the mornings, even in the pouring rain, and after school every day I had to pick him up. We caught the city bus to my mom's office, where she worked as a secretary. We hung around while she finished work. There was a gas station below her office, and she gave us money to buy snacks. I learned later that she was giving us her lunch money.

At home every evening Mom went into her bedroom, sobbed, and prayed out loud for what seemed like hours. My brother and I watched TV, trying to ignore the sound of her grief. Sometimes she was so loud and emotional that we thought she had lost her mind, and we were scared. But she always came out in a better mood, her face red and swollen as she quietly made us dinner.

Looking for Hope

I wish I could say that my behavior improved, but it actually got worse. The only emotion I knew was anger. I had grown up watching adults get angry with each other and with me—my dad, my mom, my grandfather, and my teachers. That deep well of anger inside me was always threatening to overflow. Sadness turned into anger. Disappointment turned into anger. I had no peace. Everything was swallowed up in a cauldron of black emotions.

Happiness seemed fake to me. The only time I was happy was when I was in a fight. I could punch holes in walls, kick things, and hurt people. Then I would feel exhausted and good, as if I had been able to purge something black and evil from inside me.

We still went to church, and I often went down for altar calls. The people of the church prayed over me once, almost as if performing an exorcism, just trying to help me. I don't recall that it had any effect. My mom, though changed in every way by her conversion, was desperate and did not know what to do with me. I don't remember much about it, but Mom was very happy when my brother and I were baptized in the ocean. Even that had no effect on me.

One Sunday night we were at church, and Mom asked me, "Do you have any homework to do tonight?"

I said I didn't, but I actually did. I just didn't know it because I had been kicked out of class on Friday and did not hear the assignment.

"Are you sure? I'm going to call your teacher right now," she said. Things were so bad at school by then that Mom had all my teachers' home phone numbers.

"I'm pretty sure," I told her. "I was kicked out of class so I don't know."

She called my teacher from a pay phone at the church. My teacher told her that I had been let back into class with ten minutes left, and the assignment was written on the chalkboard. I should have known it. As soon as Mom hung up the phone, she spanked me.

> That deep well of anger inside me was always threatening to overflow.

Angry and humiliated, I took off running into the darkness. Our church was in the middle of Waikiki, and I ran a few blocks and hid in some bushes. She ran after me and then enlisted everyone in the church to help. I heard them walking by, calling my name, but I stayed hidden.

When Nik came by, he happened to stick his head in the bushes and find me. "Bryan, please come back," he said through tears.

As much for his sake as anything else, I came out. Mom was so upset that she did not know what to do, so I spent the night at the pastor's house, and the pastor helped smooth things over.

That was not the worst of my behavior. At some point before or after the divorce, I started cutting myself with razors and writing suicide-themed notes. I don't know where I got the idea—maybe from movies—but it started with drawing pictures of myself hanging. I depicted myself as a stick figure with my name on it and a noose around my neck. I would say things like, "I should just kill myself." I hid these notes in a pencil box that I kept in my room.

A couple of times while I was home alone, I took my protractor and poked myself, then dragged it across my wrist as hard as I could. Another time I took a knife and put the dull side on my wrist, lightly dragging it across and wondering what it would feel like to cut myself with the sharp side. My little experiments left scratches that bled a bit and then scabbed over. Next I started taking a razor and cutting little slits in my knuckles. I don't know why I did it. Perhaps it was another way of expressing the torment I felt about the divorce. Over time the scars formed rows on my knuckles, like the lines a prisoner makes in the wall of his cell to count the years. I still have those scars on my fingers, among the dozens of other scars I got from fistfights.

Then Mom found my pencil box full of death notes. Greatly alarmed, she took me to counseling. I don't remember much about those counseling sessions except that the counselor was an older man who asked me questions while we played pick-up sticks. After evaluating me for a while, he told my mom, "If you want to save Bryan, get him involved in sports."

We had no money for me to join a private sports club, and public schools didn't offer teams at my grade level, so nothing changed. I fought other kids whenever I could: before school, after school, and at recess. I didn't make any effort at schoolwork, went reluctantly to church, listened to my mom pray for us day and night, and missed my dad terribly. Life felt so hopeless, and I wondered what might finally save us all.

THREE
HOW TRACK AND FIELD SAVED MY LIFE

Mom was always praying about something. She prayed when we drove somewhere and an ambulance passed by: "Oh, Lord, please touch the person that ambulance is going to." She prayed when we got to the mall: "Lord, please give us a parking spot close to the entrance." When an ideal spot opened up in the crowded parking lot, she thanked God for answering her prayer. Each morning I woke up and heard her praying for my brother and me, for people at the church, and for family members. When Nik and I walked by her room, she pulled us in and made us pray with her.

But I didn't believe in prayer, and I thought Mom was half-crazy. I had tried prayer: I had prayed for my parents to get back together. When that prayer went unanswered, I concluded that God only answered the prayers He wanted to answer, and so it was a waste of time to ask Him for anything. He was going to do what He wanted anyway.

I also thought my mom diminished the dignity and seriousness of prayer by praying for silly things like parking spots and passing ambulances. Even though she seemed to get results, my brother and I chalked it up to coincidence. We felt that prayer shouldn't be wasted on trivia like not walking too far at the mall; prayer should be for meaningful things. The little prayers she said throughout the day for minor things needled me.

Her main topic of prayer was always my brother and me. She reminded us constantly that she was praying for us, and we heard her crying out to God regularly in her bedroom. Her prayer habit spooked us, and we tried to ignore it as best we could. We didn't realize we were seeing the making of a prayer warrior whose petitions are probably still being answered in our lives.

One day Mom came out of her bedroom after a long time of prayer and said matter-of-factly, "God just gave me a vision of your new dad."

Nik and I looked at each other, thinking, *This lady has finally gone cuckoo.* She went on to describe the man in her vision in physical detail and ended by saying, "And he's going to give you guys cable television." That was a big promise because we badly wanted cable. We especially wanted the Disney Channel so we could watch shows like *The Wonderful World of Disney* and movies like *Newsies.* We were always asking Mom for cable.

A few months later she went on a blind date and the man she'd been paired up with matched the exact description she had given us. Not only that, but he worked for the cable company. They were married in a small home ceremony, and just as Mom had said, we got cable—for free.

Starting Over

Our new stepdad moved us to Kaneohe, on the other side of the island, in the middle of my sixth-grade year. The new marriage made things a little easier. We had a nice house. We had the stability of two adults and a steady income. And since we were farther away from Honolulu, I was able to skip some weekends working at my grandfather's shop.

But not everything improved with the new setup. My mom's and stepdad's relationship was initially rockier than they had expected, and they began to fight a lot. He had been married before, but he had no children. He wanted to be a father to my brother and me, but we weren't looking for a new dad. I was going into adolescence and didn't think I needed another authority figure in my life; I already had plenty of those. Everybody was trying to tell me what to do. I interpreted his "fathering" as attempts to control me. Plus, he was white, while my real dad was African American and my mom was Japanese. He was so different from me. It was just about the worst fit I could imagine, on a number of levels.

My stepdad was—and is—a dedicated Christian man who was always volunteering at church, and he drove around listening to Christian music, which I couldn't stand. We didn't get along from the start. Our troubled relationship was by no means his fault. I had built up a wall and wasn't going to let him into my life. He wasn't my *real* dad, even though my mom tried to force us to call him that. My brother and I at first called him "Uncle," which is how Hawaiians refer to a close male relative. My real dad had moved to the Big Island to start a new life there, and as far as I was concerned, this uncle would not be replacing him. My real dad and I still talked by phone, though I didn't see him much.

Our family started going to Hope Chapel Foursquare Church in Kaneohe, which became an important place in my young life. Many of my friends from school went there, and the youth group was considered cool. The church met in the cafeteria of my public elementary school and was so close to our house that I could walk to it. The youth pastor, Richard Ainsworth, soon became one of the biggest influences on me.

Richard was half African and half white, and he changed my world, maybe not noticeably at first but profoundly over time. I was still getting into a lot of trouble at school and with my parents. I felt, perhaps wrongly, that I didn't have anyone who would take the extra time to be with me one-on-one—except Rich. He came to my school and met me at lunch just to hang out. He did the same thing for a lot of kids, but it felt as if he were doing it only for me.

Rich was my closest friend for a couple of years. He did not try to parent me or give me all the answers. He just listened. Some nights things got to be too much for me, and I would run away from home. My mom and stepdad would drive around until they found me. Then they would call Rich to pick me up, and I would sleep at his house. I would vent at length about my feelings, and he patiently listened. He was gentle and soft-spoken. He could be strict and stern if he needed to be, and he got that way with me a few times, but usually he was just what I needed: a friend.

One time the situation intensified with my parents. We were fighting, and I started packing my bags, saying I was going to leave for good. Mom begged me to stay while my stepdad told me to stop resisting authority. Rich came to pick me up after school the next day. I assumed he had talked to my parents. He had his fishing poles in the back of the car, and together we went out to the ocean, into the chest-high water, and fished for a long time. He didn't have to say anything, and neither did I. That made all the difference in the world to me. It was exactly the kind of interaction I needed.

I don't know whether I would have gotten through those junior high years without Rich. I saw him on Sundays and throughout the week, and we had Friday night services at the school. He invited me to perform tasks like setting up chairs or changing the transparencies for worship time. I loved the praise I received for doing these things, and in a way I was emulating my stepdad, who often set up and put away chairs for services. I lived to hear people tell me, "Good job, Bryan. You're such a blessing." I usually got attention for doing negative things, but getting attention for doing positive things was even better.

At church I was a different person. I thought I was tougher than anyone else, and I wasn't afraid to get into fights, but the kids were different, so I could let down my guard and have real

Richard . . . changed my world, maybe not noticeably at first but profoundly over time.

fun. We played the kinds of games that boys like, and Rich was good about letting us be active without letting us be rough. I felt safe there, and Hope Chapel became like a second home to me.

But at school I was still fighting and being disruptive. I avoided all homework, so my grades suffered. I smoked cigarettes that other students brought to school, and I stole liquor from stores. Over time these habits got worse.

One time a blond kid, a little bit of a punk, was playing soccer with us at recess. Then he grabbed the ball and said, "Let's play rugby!" I said, "No! Put the ball down. We're in the middle of a game." I started chasing him and yanked the ball from his hand, put it on the ground, and started playing soccer again. He came up behind me to grab the ball, and when he did, I pulled it back, and somehow he flipped over onto the ground. I started punching him, and something in the whole process gave him a concussion. His parents were very unhappy, and the principal gave me five days of in-school suspension. But I didn't care. I was going to fight with whomever I wanted, whenever I wanted.

That included fighting with teachers. In sixth grade we were doing an essay assignment and learning to write with pens. I made a mistake but had neglected to bring my bottle of Wite-Out. I asked people around me for their Wite-Out, but the teacher protested.

"You can't borrow someone else's," he said. "If you didn't bring your own, you're out of luck."

"But I'm trying to do the assignment," I replied.

"Give it back," he insisted.

I didn't obey. I used the Wite-Out and then gave it back.

"That's it. Go stand outside," he ordered.

"No, I'm going to finish my assignment," I said.

"Then come up front," he demanded.

When I did, he took my paper and wrote a big F on it in front of everybody. I was so upset that I took a swing at him. He ducked, and I hit the chalkboard instead, breaking a bone in my hand. The teacher sent me to the principal's office, and I was suspended again.

My hand swelled up, and the school nurse wrapped it, but I never had a doctor treat it. It healed up on its own, more or less, but to this day that bone feels strange. When my mom saw what I had done, she said simply, "You deserve it."

I threatened another teacher in eighth grade, telling her, "You're lucky you're my teacher and we're not outside, or else I'd beat you up." I was suspended from school for nine days. The first day back, I got into a fight with another student and was suspended again. I didn't even consider changing my behavior for the better.

I did have some rare good interactions with teachers, one of which became a milestone for me. I was in sixth grade, and I was better than all the other kids in athletics. I could win almost every game. It felt effortless to me. So the only sure A on my report card came in PE. It was as close to a guarantee as I had. But Mr. Awa, my PE teacher, gave me a failing grade. It was devastating and completely unexpected.

Instead of avoiding me or blowing me off as some teachers would have done, he asked to meet with me after class. He sat me down and said, "Bryan, I failed you, yes. Your parents are going to be upset, but you'll survive. This is not the end of your world. You're going to go on and be all right. You'll make it."

Then he explained why he failed me. Even though I was angry at him, I listened as he walked me through his reasoning. "I gave you an F not because I don't like you," he said. "It's because I care about you. I have to let you know that you can't get by just on athletics. There is more to life than playing sports." In his PE class he required more than play; he required us to research and write reports on the different sports. He even gave us tests. But I didn't study for the tests or do the reports. I thought I could pass PE by being good on the court or the field.

I don't remember many of my teachers, but I will never forget Mr. Awa because he taught me an important lesson. He was one of the few willing to risk making me angry so he could teach me something. I didn't follow his advice right away, but it remained in the back of my mind for years. Eventually I acted on it.

Discovering Track and Field

Mom kept praying as if it were going out of style, and her prayers became more specific and, in my mind, weird.

"I was praying today, and the Lord told me that He has the perfect person for your wife," she would say. "So I prayed for her today and for your children."

She said this a number of times, and I always thought, *You prayed for someone you don't know? You prayed for my wife? And my kids? I'm in eighth grade! There is something seriously wrong with you.*

But she didn't stop. "Don't doubt it, Bryan," she said. "God told me." And that was that as far as she was concerned.

Mom's new marriage had finally given her the opportunity and the money to do what the counselor had recommended: put me in organized sports. She was still desperate for a solution to help me get my life in order, and she would ask God all the time to show her a positive path for me. One day when I was in sixth grade, she sat me down and said with a sense of finality and decision, "Bryan, you're going to play sports. You can run track and field, or you can swim."

My first response was, "Aw! I want to play football."

She said, "Too bad. Track and field and swimming are the only sports where you don't have the opportunity to put your hands on anybody else, so you won't get into fights."

I thought about my choice. I knew I was a pretty fast runner, but I was also good at swimming. We were at the beach all the time. After some consideration, I chose track and field, in part because I didn't want to wear an embarrassing little swimsuit and in part because I knew how good running made me feel.

I joined the Kailua Track Club coached by Duncan Macdonald, an Olympic 5000-meter runner in the 1976 Montreal games. My parents took me to my first practice at the Kailua High School track, and I was nervous. I didn't know what clothes or shoes to wear, and I didn't know what to expect. All I knew was that I was going to run.

> One day when I was in sixth grade, she sat me down and said . . . , "Bryan, you're going to play sports."

Twenty or so kids were gathered on the dirt track that had a little set of bleachers nearby. The field was covered in patchy grass. My mom and stepdad stayed and watched me. They were at nearly every practice and every track meet. My mom sat in the bleachers, talked to the other parents—and made sure I didn't get into trouble.

As nervous as I was, I thought I was invincible when it came to competing. I thought I was the fastest person on the planet, but very quickly I realized I wasn't. Being on the track team was going to require more than racing all day. Actual work was involved—doing drills, training, learning, and listening. That was an eye-opener for me, and initially I wasn't prepared to do any of it.

Every day we did two warm-up laps, which I thought was a lot at first, and then a whole regimen of drills. Practice was fun but hard. I enjoyed it so much that I made myself listen more than usual, and I forced myself to sit still and not horse around too much. I quickly realized that I had to either stick with the program or get out. I was willing to do the work because from the start, track felt like something that was mine, something I could do well. I didn't want it to be taken away, so I did what I had to and stayed in line. I knew I had found something more special than anything else in my life up to that point. I didn't want to blow it.

Duncan and the other coaches did a good job of keeping it fun. There was nothing of the drill sergeant in Duncan, who was a tall skinny guy with a thick mustache. He was passionate about track, and our excitement about running started at the top with him. His assistant coaches were excited. His wife was excited, and his two daughters, who later had collegiate running careers, were excited. It all added up to a great time.

One time we ran an 800, and Duncan jumped in the race with us. I

> I knew I had found something more special than anything else in my life up to that point. I didn't want to blow it.

was doing pretty well but was starting to tie up on the last lap. Duncan came up beside me, looked at me, made the Road Runner beeping sound, then took off and smoked us to the finish line. He still had it.

Duncan gave us the freedom to try whatever looked like fun. If I saw people trying the triple jump, I could say, "Hey, Coach, could I try triple jump?" He would say, "Finish this up and then you can." I'd run over there and give it a go. We were free to discover which events we liked most; then at the meets on Saturdays, we could say, "Can I run this race or do that event?" And he would enter us into the event.

The meets involved people of all ages, from those younger than me all the way up to the master's level, the older guys who came out to run. We would get ribbons in our age group. When I first started competing, I usually got fifth, sixth, or seventh place. I was not the best guy out there. But I was determined to improve and also try the long jump, triple jump, high jump, and all the sprints and running events. I didn't want to try the pole vault or throw the shot put, discus, or javelin because I was less interested in throwing and more interested in running fast and jumping high.

My competitive side was nurtured and directed by going up against other athletes. I remember racing in the 100-meter dash (known simply as "the hundred" to competitors, coaches, and fans) and not coming in first at one particular meet. I was upset and wanted to try it again. *I might not get it the first time*, I thought, *but I'll keep trying, and at some point I'm going to get it. Next time I'll do better.* I came back week after week because I wanted to win.

I didn't win much in my first year; it was more a time of getting to know the sport. But by eighth grade I was doing well, and track had come to define who I was, in my social life and in my self-conception. I enjoyed it thoroughly. I could walk around the track with my chest puffed out, and other kids would say, "Whoa, he's really fast."

Running had never been used as a negative in my life as it was for some people. In other contexts, running was a punishment. If you were a football player and fumbled the ball, the coach might make you run laps. If you didn't dress out for PE, the teacher might make you run the track.

For me, track was all positive. When I ran, my head was clear. It gave me space to think through things in my life. Later I would liken it to Eric Liddell's quote in *Chariots of Fire*: "When I run, I feel His pleasure." That feeling grew as I got older and more competitive. When I ran, everything felt good and in order.

We continued to drive to Kailua every day during the summers for club track practice. During the school year, I did not run at all because my junior high school did not have a team. The only exercise I got was in PE and at recess. But during club season, I developed more and more. I got to know my fellow teammates and made good friendships. I also got to know which guys were the fastest runners among our competitors, and I memorized their times. Those times became my standards, and I wanted to beat them. I did not like coming in second. I had developed a taste for coming across the finish line with all eyes on me, and everyone in the stands saying, "That was cool. He did a great job." I liked having everybody pat me on the back. It was an immediate, tangible way to know that the work I had put in was worth it.

Because of Duncan, I knew that if I practiced harder, I could run even faster. I saw the improvements accumulate over the weeks

I came back week after week because I wanted to win.

and years—I was getting faster, jumping higher and farther. The incentive was there for me, and the better I got, the more I started to believe in myself, to have self-worth, to want to be the best. My competitiveness took over, and I channeled my energy into finding out how good I could be.

In the fall of my ninth grade year, I started running cross country for the high school team, and from that point on I ran all year long: cross country in the fall, track in the spring, and club track in the summer. Cross country was different, and I didn't like it as much. It involved lots of long-distance running, hills, and repeat 800s, none of which I was used to. I did okay, but I wasn't the best. I did it because it got me out of the house, let me hang around with my friends—and helped me get in shape for track season. I did well that spring in track, qualifying for the state meet in the 100.

The coach of the high school cross country and track teams was Martin Hee, a local firefighter and kidney transplant recipient. He competed in the Police-Fire Games and the Transplant Games. He was an outstanding person. I soon became great friends with him and his wife, and his coaching and his personal example helped lay the foundations for my track career. We spent hours together at practice. He became like a father to me, and his wife, like a mother. My family went to his house for barbecues. In Hawaii we have what we call *ohana*, which is like an extended family. It includes not just your blood relatives but everyone who is an important part of your community. The term implies intimacy, respect, and strong bonds. The Hees were a big part of my *ohana*.

Still Struggling

My success on the track didn't transfer to school. I was still getting into trouble, fighting at lunchtime and after school. The year before, my friends and I had hung around the bottom of the stairs on a certain part of campus. We weren't supposed to leave campus, but we cut school regularly anyway. We sneaked down through the overgrown trails to the Kaneohe Bay beach before school, drank the alcohol someone managed to bring from home, and smoked cigarettes or chewed tobacco. Then we would come to school wasted, which I had been doing fairly regularly since seventh grade. I would sit in the back of class, put my head down, and fall asleep. I'm sure my teachers thought, *Thank God. Maybe he won't cause problems today.* After I was in high school, I added marijuana to this list of vices, smoking and selling it whenever I could.

My mom and stepdad were still getting into awful fights, but they happened less frequently. One day while I was at a friend's house, I suddenly had a feeling that I should go home. I tried to ignore it for a little while, but finally it was too much. I walked back home, and as I approached the front door, I could hear my mom screaming.

I ran in and found my mom and my stepdad yelling at each other. I ran toward him and pushed him against the wall. He turned and pinned me by the neck against the wall, but I wasn't afraid in the slightest. I thought, *You have no idea. I could kill you in your sleep. Who do you think you are? That's my mom you're dealing with.* I was enraged, but I did not fight back, out of respect for my mom.

Later on, however, I did fight back. It was one of those times I had been grounded from using the telephone. Since I usually got home before my parents, I was home alone when the phone rang, and I answered it. Someone wanted to speak to my mom. I told the caller she wasn't at home, and that was the end of it. My stepdad worked in the area and would periodically drop by the house. This was one of those days. When he walked in the door and saw me on the phone, he demanded to know, "What were you doing on the phone?"

"I was taking a call for Mom," I said.

"But you're grounded from the phone," he reminded me.

"I was doing something good. I was answering one of her calls," I said.

Our argument escalated until we were screaming at each other. I stomped into my room, and he followed me and got in my face. I said something that provoked him even more, and he held up his fist and said, "If you say one more word, I'll shut you up myself."

I had had enough.

"You want to fight?" I said. "Come on! Let's do it!"

I went outside to the carport and stood there cussing at him, daring him to come outside. He stood in my room, looking at me through the window and saying, "Get back in the house." Finally I went back inside. He kept yelling at me and holding his fist in my face.

"I dare you to hit me," I intended to say, but I don't remember whether I said all the words aloud because I blacked out. He had taken me up on my offer.

The next thing I remember, I was holding his face down on my bed, and there was blood all over the sheets. He was screaming, "I'm going to kill you!" I realized that something had happened, something I didn't remember, something violent. I panicked.

"You're bleeding. I'm sorry," I said.

He was screaming and trying to get away, but I was on his back. I had a lot of experience at fighting; it was one of my pastimes. But that was the first time I had blacked out. I was afraid because he seemed to be really hurt.

"If I let you go, will you calm down?" I asked.

"Yes," he said. So I let him up. There was blood all over his face.

Crying, I fell into the corner while he went into the bathroom, turned on the water, and washed his face. The terrible energy of the situation seemed to drain away.

Then he came back. "Son," he said calmly, "you need to stop crying and be a man. We had a disagreement. We got into a fight. It doesn't mean I don't love you. It's going to be okay. We'll work through it."

He went back into the bathroom, and I followed him. He was

putting a butterfly bandage on his eye. Seeing the cuts on his face, I started crying again, and I apologized to him over and over.

"Bryan," he said, "it happens. We're just going to have to deal with it."

I was certain my mom was going to kill me. Just then there was a knock at the front door.

"Police," a muffled voice said through the door.

I had already been in trouble with the police here and there. Now they were at my front door, and my stepdad was cut up, black-and-blue, his eyes bloodshot. I was sure they would take me to jail for battery. I was shaking.

My stepdad opened the door, and I was standing behind him.

"We got a domestic violence call. Is everything okay?" the officer asked.

"Everything's okay, officer," my stepdad said. "Me and my son just got into a little scuffle. But everything's okay now."

They opened the screen door and peered in.

"Are you sure everything's okay?" they said, scrutinizing his appearance. I think it helped that I looked fine, and I was the minor in the situation.

"The problem's over," my stepdad said. "We're fine."

The police left, and I sat on the couch, waiting for my mom to come home. As soon as she walked in, she could tell something was wrong.

"What happened?" she said.

"We got into a fight," I replied.

"What is going on? I cannot believe this," she said. "Tell me what happened."

"He hit me, and then I hit him," I said.

Just then he walked around the corner, looking beat-up but otherwise happy. She took it all in for a moment—his bandages and cuts, our apparent peace.

"Good for both of you!" she said angrily, then stormed into her room and slammed the door.

That was the only time we came to blows. I was afraid for it to happen again, afraid to lose control, so I held myself back. But the incident also made me feel like a man. I felt that if anything happened between my stepdad and my mom or brother, I was capable of stepping in. I could protect them, though in reality they did not need protection from him. I had proven something to myself, if not in the best way. After that, he and I still yelled at each other, but things never got to that physical level again.

Our relationship improved a bit later in my high school years. I began to respect him for what he had done for my family. In spite of everything that we had been through—the fights, the hardship between him and my mom, all my misbehavior—he never left. He was always there, paying the bills, working hard. We never went without. He was in the marriage for better or worse. Those were things I had never seen before. Not once did I think he might say, "Things are getting bad here. You guys are not my kids. You do whatever you want to. I don't want anything to do with you. I'm not paying for any of your stuff anymore." As a father myself now, I respect even more that he stayed and put up with me. He taught me that there is no compromise and that if I believe in something, I should do it wholeheartedly.

We were still going to Hope Chapel, but Richard Ainsworth had moved on to another church, and I had lost a critical connection to the things of God. I enjoyed going to church and sincerely desired to be free of my terrible pattern of drinking, smoking marijuana, and fighting. It was almost as if I had two lives—my church life and my school life—and they had nothing to do with each other. I felt guilty about my behavior only when I was at church and church camp. We would sit around the campfire up in the mountains, and I would say the prayer a thousand times: "Lord, forgive me for everything I've done. Please come into my heart." I would start crying. I knew that what I was doing was wrong. I was a sad and angry kid. I always hoped the prayer and my renewed commitment would work, and when I was up at camp and away from life, it seemed easy. I would have a great time, come back home on fire for God and ready to go, but that would last about a day before I was back into my old habits. I had a reputation to uphold as a big man on campus, a rebel, and a fighter.

Track became my escape. Mr. Hee gave me advice one time when I came to the track unsettled. Knowing that I was having all sorts of trouble with my parents and at school, he told me, "When you enter that fence around the track, everything stays outside. It will all be there when you go back out. But when you're here, you don't have to think about it." I sensed he was right. There was no point in bringing life to the track. There was nothing I could do to change it while I was running, so I might as well leave it there, run, and then pick it back up after practice.

I took his words to heart. When I got to the track, I didn't think about anything else. That habit became important to my career. I learned to build walls between different parts of my life. I could take what I was feeling and set it aside when I had to perform. I didn't realize it then, but it is a critical skill for a decathlete because you are constantly moving from one event, one success or failure, to the next opportunity.

As I went through high school, track became my lifeline, my oasis. I would go to practice, leave everything in my life at the fence, and run.

Learning from a Champion

The summer before my sophomore year, I went to a track camp on the island and met an Olympic-level decathlete named Chris Huffins.

Chris would go on to win a gold medal in the 1999 Pan American Games and a bronze medal at the 2000 Olympics in Sydney. During the 1996 U.S. Olympic Trials, he broke the world record in the decathlon 100 with a time of 10.22. For some reason, Chris and I got along really well. It was the first time I had met and spoken with a top athlete who was still competing.

We did drills, like A-skips and B-skips, and worked on running form: lifting your knees up, correcting running posture, and perfecting the angle of your foot strike on the ground. Drills get you accustomed to a repetitive motion so it becomes second nature. You fine-tune your running motion in training because you can't fine-tune anything during a sprint. I began to learn that track is about training and repetition, doing something until it becomes natural.

I learned a lot from Chris during camp, especially about how to work on my running form. I also watched him do his workout, and I met his girlfriend. After camp he drove me to my house. As I was about to get out of the car, he happened to look at my shoes, which were all torn up and had holes in the sides.

"Don't you have some new shoes?" he asked.

"No," I said.

Right there in the car he took his shoes off and handed them to me. They were Mizunos that had his name embroidered on them.

"Here, you can have these," he said.

His gift was the coolest thing ever. I had never been given anything like that before. They were the right size and fit. More than that, his act of kindness told me he thought I was good enough. I wore them for years until they literally fell apart.

Another helpful influence in my life at the time was a college athlete named Jumanne Washington, one of the best runners in Hawaii. He was a very good sprinter who ran the 100 in 10.30 and the 400 in 45 seconds flat. He had gotten a scholarship to a major university but was back in Hawaii temporarily. He shared some techniques he thought I should try. I was hungry for the knowledge and grateful to pick up skills from him. And I was just cocky enough to think I could beat him someday.

Back at school I ran cross country in the fall and track in the spring. I qualified again for the state championships in the 100 but didn't do well at the meet. That summer track camp was held on Maui, and quite a few more people were there, including sprinter Chryste Gaines, the leadoff runner on the gold medal U.S. 4 x 100-meters team at the 1996 Olympics in Atlanta; and Jan Johnson, a 1972 Olympic bronze medalist and National Pole Vault Hall of Fame member. Chris Huffins gave a talk on sprinting mechanics and showed us a bunch of slides.

His act of kindness told me he thought I was good enough.

By that time Chris and I were friendly and even talked a little trash to each other. I had attended a sprinting lecture that day and was feeling confident. After the slide show, everybody was going to various events. "Why don't you try the vault?" Chris suggested to me. So I ran over and did the pole vault session. I had no idea that Jan Johnson was one of the all-time gurus of the sport. We did drills on how to take off, which hand to hold the pole in, all the basic stuff I had never learned before. I loved every minute of it.

After that I went back to Chris, and he said, "Why don't you try the hurdles?" So I did that, and then he suggested I go with him to a throws practice. We had a friendly throw competition, and he offered to spot me 4 meters (a little more than 13 feet) because I had never thrown a shot put before. He showed me a little bit of technique, and then I stepped up and threw the sixteen-pound shot a little more than 12 meters (more than 39 feet), which is amazing for a first throw. Suddenly he realized that to beat me, he had to throw 16-plus meters (more than 52 feet), which for a decathlete is a world-class distance. He came up short, and because of the handicap, I beat him, which energized me even more. Of course, I'm pretty sure I committed fouls during my throw that Chris didn't mention.

"You should try doing a few more events this year and let me know how you do," he said as we parted.

I took that advice and, going into my junior year, expected to do well. I was going to be competing at the varsity level, and my goal was to win events at the state championships. I ran cross country for the last time and did well at state with a decent time of 17 minutes for 3 miles. But from then on I dropped distance running and focused solely on track.

I won meets in the spring and performed very well for the whole track season. My times were faster than ever. By now I was thinking beyond what other athletes in Hawaii were doing and looking to what athletes in California and Texas were doing. I knew there was a bigger picture. I subscribed to *Track & Field News* and looked through it to see how everyone performed at state meets and who the standout runners were nationally. The top high school runners were running 10.50 and 10.40 in the 100, so that's what I wanted to do. At the time, I was running it in 10.80 or so, and I thought I could get close to their times. Yet I was naturally pessimistic about ever competing nationally and nervous about competing against them. I just thought I would give it a shot and see how it went.

Without really thinking about it, I became a student of the sport. I watched other people on the track to see how they ran and jumped. I am a visual person, and if I saw someone jump far, I noted what he did differently from what I did. I recorded track meets on television and watched the other athletes before popping in one of my practice videotapes and watching myself. Then I would go out to the track and do what they did so that I could improve my form. I bought videos of running mechanics. I knew that if people were running faster than I was and I wanted to run as fast as they did, I should emulate their form. I broke their techniques down, move by move.

I was building a work ethic by watching the videos and training. I was by far the most dedicated member of the track team, and I saw my times march slowly downward, from 10.87 in the 100 to 10.84, then 10.83, then 10.78. Every time I improved, it fed the hunger to keep going. *Okay*, I thought, *I ran 10.78. Now I'll try 10.75.* I paid attention only to the next small goal. Each one caused me to pick up the intensity and work harder.

Low Expectations

Though my track work was taking off, I had no aspirations for a career in the sport. My idea of a career was to work at a convenience store or at some other nonprofessional job because then I would have freedom to go to the beach every day. I didn't think I would ever leave Hawaii. I daydreamed about having a friend who had a connection to a roofing company or something so I could get a roofing job. I wasn't afraid to work; I had grown up working with my grandfather. But my idea was to work as little as possible to make my lifestyle happen.

Having a future in sports didn't occur to me. Track gave me something to do, and it was something I liked. It met my needs at the time: the need to be good at something, to be affirmed, to be popular at school. It gave me something to identify with. Competing for God's glory or being a positive influence was far from my mind. It came down to the fact that track and field was the only thing that consistently gave me a good feeling. It was also the only thing keeping my head above water. Track had become my lifeboat, my private passion, and part of my persona—and yet I didn't love the sport for what it was; I loved it only for what it gave me.

At some point I latched onto the goal, at least publicly, of competing in the Olympics. In high school I signed yearbooks with the Olympic rings and "2004." I wrote it only because it fit my reputation. I had already been voted Most Athletic. If I didn't make it to the Olympics, nobody would care. I kept the idea active in people's minds because it kept me popular. But I never thought it would actually happen. Not only were my times nowhere near the national marks—was it even physically possible for me to run the 100 in 10.31?—but everything in my life had taught me that dreams don't come true. If life gives you lemons, you don't make lemonade—you learn to like lemons.

Mom thought otherwise. She had continued praying for me, and as I entered high school, she repeatedly told me: "God's got a plan for your life. He's got something special in your future. I know it. He's told me. I prayed about it." Then she became more specific: "You're going to go to the Olympics and win the gold medal. God told me so. I don't want to hear any doubt about it, no negative talk, no negative feelings. God has shown me that you're going to win the gold medal."

I never believed her, and I hated hearing her say it. I was skeptical that God had told her anything.

She also said, "You're a leader, whether you want to be or not. You don't have a choice. You are destined for something great. God has a plan for your life, and He's not going to let you screw it up."

We argued about that. I would say, "I don't want to be a leader. I want to do what I want to do. I want to get into trouble, smoke weed, and drink."

She didn't accept that: "I'm sorry. You don't get to choose. You're a leader, and that's just how it is. God has a special plan for you. That's why you will always get caught when you're doing things you shouldn't do. God is not going to allow you to screw this up."

Her comments infuriated me. I didn't want the responsibility of being an example for anyone. I didn't want to give up anything for my sport. I wanted to go out with friends on Friday night and party, and then compete in a track meet on Saturday.

My mom was unrelenting. I would ask to go to the movies, and she would turn me down because I had a track meet the next day. She reminded me that I had made a commitment to my team and my coaches. I needed to make sure I was at my best and ready to compete. Those were the nights I would end up quitting the team. If I couldn't have fun, I didn't want any part of it. She would say, "If you're going to quit the track team, then you call your coach and tell him." So I would call Coach Hee and say, "Coach, I'm quitting the track team. I'm not coming out tomorrow," and then hang up.

A few days later I would feel stupid because I had given up the only thing that made me special, just to spite my mother. So I would talk to Coach Hee,

> "God is not going to allow you to screw this up."

and in his gentle way he would say, "Why don't you just come out to the track, and we'll talk tomorrow." And I would go and be back on the team.

Eventually I started giving up some things voluntarily for track. I quit going to late movies before meets and gave up afternoons for practice. In my junior year my 4 x 400-meters relay teammates went to the prom instead of going to the state meet, so I was the only one there. I knew I wasn't good on a national level, but I knew I was good in Hawaii. Everyone in the track and field world in the state knew who I was. I was winning at meets and building a name for myself. I was the best in the state in many events. I don't remember losing much that year. At state championships I won three of the four events

I competed in: the 100-, 200-, and 110-meter hurdles. I got second place in the long jump.

That summer I went back to track camp and reported to Chris how I had done. He was excited and couldn't believe I had performed as well as I did, especially in the hurdles. He said to somebody who was there, "Can you believe he ran this and this in his first year of doing hurdles?" My chest swelled with pride.

"Keep it up," he told me. But he needn't have said that. I was already starting to see small glimmers of a future for me beyond the islands—and track was going to be my way out.

FOUR
SEIZING THE FUTURE

My family was at the Hees' house for a barbecue, and Mr. Hee and my stepdad got into an argument about my future. It was specifically about my grades, which were probably not good enough to get me into college. My stepdad was a realist. He knew athletic scholarships were difficult to come by, and having good grades was the one sure way to get into college. Mr. Hee finally told him, "He's going to get a scholarship. Don't worry about it. If he doesn't, I'll pay for him to go to school myself."

As it turned out, he was right. During the summer after my junior year, letters from big universities started arriving in my mailbox. Cornell, the University of Arkansas, and many others pursued me. Each was interested in having me attend on an athletic scholarship. Up to then I'd had no ambition to attend college or leave the islands. I had floated through life being very happy with mediocrity. I did just enough to keep people off my back. Getting a C out of a class was fine with me. In fact, it was preferable because it meant I had not wasted too much time studying.

But as the letters piled up, I began to think that maybe going away to college would be fun. At the very least I would get away from my parents for a while and have a chance to really party. Even if I did attend college somewhere, I did not believe I would ever finish; I was convinced that I did not have it in me academically.

The other people in my *ohana*—my mom, my stepdad, Mr. Hee, and Chris Huffins—were taking my future more seriously than I was. At one point before my senior year, Chris and I talked.

"I have the perfect school for you," he said.

"What is it?" I asked.

"Don't worry about it. If I told you, you wouldn't know it anyway."

But I was insistent and kept asking him.

Finally he told me: "It's called Azusa Pacific University."

"What?" I had never heard of it, and it sounded lame.

"It's a small Christian university, so your mom will love it, and it's got a great track program, so it will be good for you."

There was no chance I would go there, especially since I was getting a lot of interest from Division I schools. But I went home and mentioned it to my mom, who must have done some research on the Internet because the next thing I knew she was talking about Azusa (APU) all the time. "Bryan," she would say, "this is the school for you. This is where you need to be."

I didn't pay much attention to her. I had a nominal relationship with God, but it was mainly through my parents. I had recommitted my life at every youth camp, and I'd had life-changing experiences with Richard Ainsworth. But I was at a place in my life where I did not want to do the Christian thing anymore. I wanted to go my own way.

APU, however, kept popping up. Kevin Reid, APU's track coach, got in touch with me and e-mailed me throughout the year. A lot of other coaches sent e-mails, too, so that was nothing unusual. Kevin asked me to keep him posted on my results after every track meet. I obliged, but I felt I was just humoring him. The parties, the fun, the big time were going to be at a Division I school, and that's where I was headed.

Big Man on Campus

Even though I ran club track that summer, I skipped cross country in the fall of my senior year and used that time to train for track. A guy from Canada was living on the islands, a former Olympian named Dacre Bowen. He coached track at a private school and did one-on-one coaching on the side. I heard about him and decided to try him out. I started catching the bus and riding half an hour after school every day to meet with him. He had me doing pull-ups, push-ups, and track workouts.

When track season came around, I was ready to compete. I even had a set of new personal routines. I went to the track with my earphones in, ignored everyone else, and went through my warm-ups. People thought I was cocky, but it wasn't that. Other kids might be out there just having fun, but to me, track was life. If I worked hard, I could be good. If I didn't work hard, I wouldn't be good. In a life full of things I couldn't control, I could control this.

That year I competed in four events at the state meet and won all of them, breaking four state records and tying for second in the team standings—by myself. I had scored more points than most teams did. By then local newspaper and television news reports featured me. Everybody at school knew I was getting letters from major colleges. I kept talking up the idea of going to the Olympics. I even brought my dismal grades up to As and Bs so my GPA would be above 2.0, a requirement to attend a Division I school. My parents pushed me to study for the SAT, and I scored just high enough to be eligible for the NCAA.

Maybe I do have a chance to take a positive step forward. Maybe I could go to college after all. Maybe I could handle it athletically and academically. I thought about it a lot and took it seriously for the first time.

But the better I performed, the less I wanted to go to some rinky-dink Christian university.

"If I'm this good, I'm going to a Division I school," I would tell my mom.

"No, no, no," she would say. "You should go to APU. I prayed about it. It's a good school. It has what you need."

"Look," I'd tell her, "I'm the one who worked hard. I'm the one who runs track. You're not paying for college, so you don't have a say. I'll go wherever I want."

> That year I competed in four events at the state meet and won all of them, breaking four state records and tying for second in the team standings— by myself.

This argument continued throughout my senior year. I kept e-mailing Kevin my results, and with all the letters coming from schools of all kinds, I felt like the baddest person on the planet. I still got into trouble at school, but it didn't happen nearly as often. One day I used a big fat Sharpie to draw graffiti on the school bathroom wall and mirror and signed it with my tag name: Icon. As I walked out the door and put the Sharpie in my pocket, the principal walked into the bathroom. When he saw the graffiti, he turned right around and nabbed me.

That same night I was supposed to receive the Athlete of the Year award at a school banquet, but I wasn't allowed to go. For the first time I realized how my behavior off the track could affect my sport. I thought, *Man, I really screwed that one up. I was going to be honored as a big guy on campus.* My mom and dad were upset that I had spoiled it for myself.

Changing Direction

As my senior year went on, my mom kept pleading, "Please, just go look at APU."

"No," I said repeatedly. But she kept praying and praying and bringing it up constantly, so finally I relented.

"Okay," I said. "I will take a look at this school, but after I've checked it out, I'm coming back home. Once I make my decision, that's it. I don't want to hear anything else about it."

She agreed. God would have to take care of the rest and speak to me the way He apparently had spoken to her.

APU was not a completely off-the-wall choice. It had a world-class track program, even if it didn't have the size and prestige of other schools. Dave Johnson, bronze medalist at the 1992 Olympics, was an APU alum. All the Reebok commercials featuring Dan and Dave were filmed on the APU campus. The Visa decathlon team, which included Chris Huffins, trained there; that was why he knew the coaches. NFL player Christian Okoye had gone there and competed in discus, shot put, and hammer throw, and he still held a record eight individual titles in the conference. Olympic athletes Davidson Ezinwa and Innocent Egbunike went to APU too.

I set up a trip to visit the campus and take a look at the program, but I was immediately turned off when I learned the school couldn't pay for my airline ticket. Other schools offered to fly me out, put me up, show me a good time, take me to great parties, and introduce me to girls. That was the lifestyle I wanted. What would I do at a boring, small, Christian school? There wouldn't be fun parties. That was for sure. I couldn't imagine there being any decent girls. But I kept my promise to my mom and flew to Los Angeles with her and my stepdad. Kevin had gotten the school to cover our hotel cost for the three days we were there, which seemed like the least it could do.

We drove onto the APU campus the morning after we arrived. It was a big moment for me because it was my first time on a college campus. I had been to the University of Hawaii track but never through the main campus. APU felt cool and grown-up, nothing at all like high school. We walked over to the recruiting office to let them know we were on campus, and they directed us to Kevin's office. There we met him in person. But whatever ceremony or big welcome I had been expecting did not happen, and he didn't seem to be in a hurry to impress us.

"Feel free to walk around the campus," he said after taking us to lunch at a local Hawaiian restaurant with a couple of other athletes. "We've got practice later today if you want to come by."

Whatever ideas I had about being a pampered athlete did not materialize at APU. But I was intrigued by the whole scene, which was so new to me. We left his office, walked around campus, and dropped by the dorms, where I was introduced to some guys on the track team. When I saw they were living there without parents and had cars so they could get around, I was more impressed. I loved the idea of living with a bunch of guys and nobody telling us what to do. That was a big draw, but that would be true anywhere.

That afternoon I attended practice with the team and ran into a friend of mine who'd gone to church with me for a long time. She was a goalie for the soccer team now. I hung out with her after practice and ended up staying on campus with the guys while my parents went back to the hotel. One student had an early DVD release of the movie *Titanic* because her dad worked in the movie industry, so a bunch of us watched it in the dorm.

When we were leaving, they told me to be careful not to let the resident adviser see us. I had never heard of the rule that guys and girls weren't supposed to socialize in their dorms past a certain hour. Almost on cue, the RA caught us. I didn't even go to the school, and I was already breaking the rules, although without knowing it at the time. There wasn't any punishment for me because I was just a potential recruit.

During the next few days my family and I continued to look around and see what the school was like. We even went to a chapel service. As we prepared to leave, I realized that in spite of myself, I felt comfortable at APU. Something about it felt like home, like Hawaii. It was small and familiar in the same way. The atmosphere was relaxed. I still wasn't impressed by the size or scale or partying ambitions of the place. Nobody shoved girls at me, took me out on the town, or slipped money to me. But before I left campus to go back home, I signed a letter of intent and told Kevin I would love to come there.

Back at home I canceled plans of going to other schools. I still don't know why I did it. I did not have a change of heart. I did not suddenly become a better person. All I can think is, God put His hands around me and directed me there. Maybe it was His way of not letting me screw up the plan He had for me.

There was no decathlon at the high school level in Hawaii, probably because we were not allowed to throw the javelin. The summer before I went to APU, I did my first decathlon on the grass in Hawaii just to qualify for the Junior Olympics in Seattle. I had never done the throws or pole vault in a competition before that qualifying event and had little to no opportunity to practice, but I did well enough to qualify. I was on my way to Seattle.

My future coach, Kevin Reid, came to watch. Another future

APU decathlete, Matt Norquist, was there, too, and we became fast friends. It was an unusually hot and sunny day for Seattle. Some guys in the stands were shirtless. I'd had a week to practice the pole vault and was able to jump 13 feet 6 inches, which I thought was impressive for a high school kid. I remember flying down the runway, planting the pole but not getting enough momentum. I went up and was hanging onto the pole as it stalled at near vertical. I curled up in a ball and shook it to try to get it to fall over the right way, toward the bar. I succeeded somehow, let go, and fell into the pit of cushions. I was laughing when I finished.

Later that day while I was running the 400, my new pair of Nike AirMax shoes was stolen, so I had to compete the second day in an old pair of shoes. I was disqualified from the 400 and ran the 1500 poorly but finished out the meet and won third place overall. I had accumulated enough points in nine events to match what the other athletes did in ten. Kevin congratulated me, and soon I would be heading to Southern California to compete for him and APU.

Even though I had committed to go to APU, I made some personal vows: I was not going to attend chapel or church unless I felt like it. I didn't care if I got kicked out of school for it. I was going to have fun, run on my scholarship, and let everybody know that I was a big man on campus. If I was going to a Christian school, I was going to do it *my* way.

All the recruiting efforts by the other universities stopped—except for the coach from California Baptist University, Rana Reider, who kept contacting me. I think he wanted to be my second choice if things didn't work out with APU, which was Cal Baptist's conference rival.

My mom was upset that he pursued me. "I don't think it's right that he's still writing to you after you've already committed," she said.

Years later Rana became one of my coaches, and he remains a key part of my Olympic training team.

Party Time

For the first two years at APU, I lived up to my commitment to party, run track, and party some more. My parents brought me over before my freshman year and dropped me off on campus with two big suitcases and boxes of my stuff. I had punched my ticket out of Hawaii. What lay ahead, I didn't know. I just hoped it was fun.

I lived in Engstrom Hall, the new dorm on campus, which had just been opened up to freshmen. Other freshmen from the track team were there, too, and we became instant buddies. My roommate was a friend from high school. Because we were from Hawaii, we soon got a reputation for eating bizarre foods that our parents sent us in care packages—nori, musubis, dried squid, and more. People looked at us as if we were from outer space as we munched on those local Hawaiian delights, but we smiled and invited them to have a bite. It was good stuff.

Any freshman with a full-ride scholarship feels like a big man on campus, especially at a place like APU where there are few full-ride scholarships. I was no different. My self-confidence went through the roof. But being alone without parents around to tell me what to do was a major shock that I was not ready for. My schedule became completely untethered from common sense. I stayed up late even though I had early classes. I partied when I should have been studying. I messed around when I should have been saving my energy for the track. I was driven along by my desire to have fun.

Wherever a good time presented itself—parties on and off campus—I was there. Once I became part of the partying clique, word traveled quickly about what was happening and where. I did class work and track practice just so I could shake free and go to the next party. But I was limited because I didn't have a car or much free cash. The scholarship didn't provide spending money, so I had to rely on friends to haul me around or give me loans. I was not about to ask my parents for help. I would have gone hungry and homeless before doing that. I had learned that taking money from someone puts you in emotional debt to him or her, and I didn't want my family to have any handle on me, to tell me what to do or to expect something from me.

My mom sent money, but I never asked for it. I actually told her not to send it. When she would remind me, "Dad and I are sending you money to get by," I'd reply, "I told you not to send it. You sent it because you wanted to do that, not because I needed it." My freedom was worth any cost.

> I messed around when I should have been saving my energy for the track.

As part of my scholarship I had a work-study job. For lack of a better description, it was sort of like being a night watchman at the track. People from the neighborhood or APU students would jog around the track at night for exercise. I was there to supervise, to make sure nobody was doing graffiti, bringing their dogs, or loitering. If someone got hurt, I was supposed to call campus safety. I don't remember doing much good. I would sit in the press box way up high and do my homework or sleep. Sometimes I wrote down that I was there when I wasn't. I did not take seriously my job responsibilities or much else in my life.

In spite of my aversion to church, I started going to chapel because the track team went as a team and sat together in the same row; it was the cool thing to do. I fell immediately into the same spiritual habits I'd had in Hawaii. I knew about God and thought I had a relationship with Him, but I was always questioning whether the relationship was real. My heart was tender, in a way, and whenever an altar call was made, I looked up, made eye contact with the speaker, and tried to recommit my life. I think when you don't make a firm commitment, you end up questioning it all the time. Growing up in the Pentecostal church, I heard a lot about backsliding, and I was pretty sure that if I was a Christian, I was backslidden. But after each chapel service I would walk out and go right back to doing what I was doing. My pattern was consistently inconsistent, if nothing else.

Trying to Keep Up

When I agreed to go to APU on a track and field scholarship to do the decathlon, I had no idea what I was getting myself into. Training for all ten events was more than I bargained for. I'm glad I was too ignorant to know better because by the time I realized it, I was already committed.

The decathlon is composed of the following events, listed here in the order in which they take place in competition:

Day One
- 100-meter dash
- long jump
- shot put
- high jump
- 400 meters

Day Two
- 110-meter hurdles
- discus throw
- pole vault
- javelin throw
- 1500 meters

The scoring system for the decathlon is different from other individual track and field events and, to outsiders, can be a little inscrutable. Athletes earn points in each individual event; these are combined into a single overall score for each athlete. The highest overall score wins. For example, if an athlete runs the 100 in 11.5 seconds, he receives 753 points. If he runs it in 10.5 seconds, he receives 975 points. The scale is not linear but exponential, awarding more points per unit of increase the higher the score. The scoring system, set by the International Association of Athletics Federations (IAAF), is designed to award equal points for equal ability (as much as that can be measured) in each event. This encourages athletes to be perfectly well-rounded and disallows "specialists" in each event from having an unfair advantage.

In most events elite performers earn between 850 and 1,000 points, meaning that most combined scores in major competitions are more than 8,000. The minimum world-class score is considered to be 8,500.

I had much to learn about the decathlon, from scoring to training. My day at APU started with classes at 7:30 a.m. I had to sign up for early ones so I could make it to practice at 2:00 p.m. We practiced from 2:00 to 6:00 p.m. or later every day. There were about thirty guys on the team, some of them new and some of them returning. There were also a few national-level decathletes practicing with us, guys who could score 8,000 points. One on the team with us was Jordan Hudgens. Two others—David Pope and Tage Peterson— were not on the team but were training with Kevin for the 2000 Olympic Trials. They ran with us, trained with us, and killed themselves on the track as they tried to rise to the level needed to win major national and international meets.

Those older guys had a great influence on us younger competitors. We looked to them to set the pace, and they set a fast one. Some of them threw 14 or 15 meters (45 to 50 feet) in the shot; I could throw only 12 (about 39 feet). Some of them could run 300 meters in

34 seconds; I was running it in 36 and then lying on the track ready to pass out while they kept walking around. Some ran a 46-second quarter mile; I ran it in 49 seconds, which is a big difference.

Instead of practicing separately, we all practiced together no matter who was better in each event. The standout athletes in each event set the standard, and we all tried to meet or exceed it. The expectation was that all of us would work hard. That's what we saw modeled, and that's what we did. As freshmen we were trying to keep up and prove we were worthy of sharing the same practice space. If they ran fast, we had to run faster. That caused them to run even faster so as not to be beaten by freshmen. We were constantly trying to one-up each other. The competition made us better. Iron sharpened iron, and the intensity was high.

My goal at first was just to keep up. Deep down I also wanted what they wanted—to compete at a higher level than collegiate athletics—but it still seemed out of reach. I had scored in the low 7,000s in my only decathlon. Ascending to an 8,000 score seemed like asking me to jump over the moon. And the true champions were scoring just under 9,000 points. That was superhuman. As confident as I played it on the outside, I had growing doubts about my future in this sport.

Competing on the college level was a big transition, physically, for me. We started lifting weights, which I had not really done in high school. And the length of practice doubled to four hours or more. More than that, my mentality toward training had to change. I wasn't training for just a few events; I was training for all of them: sprinting, jumping, hurdles, distance running, and throwing. You have to balance your approach because practicing one more than the others detracts from the other nine. Building up muscle helps you in the shot put but can hurt you in the sprints, jumps, and endurance events—the 400 and 1500. Training for the decathlon is a series of well-thought-out compromises.

We usually practiced three events a day. After practice we lifted weights and then hurried over to the cafeteria that closed at 7:00 p.m. There we would pile our trays with as much food as we could, and we spent the next hour eating. We lived at the track, and many of us hung out together off the track. We formed our own little clique. We had to. Nobody else shared our exacting schedule. Decathletes train long hours; we're always the first to arrive and the last to leave. It was easier to socialize with them than to coordinate with people who had more free time and didn't understand the demands of the sport.

Kevin was an encouraging, laid-back coach. He had been on the football and track teams at APU and then started coaching. He always told me, "You've just got to believe in yourself. You can do this." He talked each of us up and boosted our confidence. And he really believed it; he wasn't just blowing hot air. His manner was almost always calm and upbeat.

Some coaches yell and have their watch out as they run across the track and say, "Come on! You've got to pick it up!" Kevin would simply say, "Today we're going to run this workout, and this is the time you need to do. Ready, go." He would hit the stopwatch, watch us run around the track, then read off the times when we crossed the finish line and say, "Good job, guys." He was more Phil Jackson than Bobby Knight. He would tell us: "You guys know what you need to do, and it's up to you to do it." If people weren't responding, he might get a little louder but not much louder and not that often. His attitude with us was, "I'm not going to hold your hand. Either you want to be out here, or you don't. If you do, do what you need to do."

Kevin's system emphasized fitness and strength over immediate results and perfect technique. He believed that the fitter and stronger we were, the better we would perform over time; everything would catch up. But my initial results were terrible. I had a lot of trouble learning the new events. My body was in shock from training differently and being broken down so it could be rebuilt. I struggled with the hurdles because they were three inches higher than in high school. I hit my trail-leg ankle so many times on the hurdles that it scarred and calcified; it looks swollen and feels tender to this day.

I also put on a lot of weight from lifting and maturing. I came in at about 165 pounds and got up to 180. I was not used to all the new weight, and my events suffered because of it. I couldn't run as fast or jump as high and far as I had in high school. In high school I could run the 100 in 10.50. For most of my freshman year in college I didn't run that. The long jump was especially frustrating. In high school I didn't have any long jump competition under 7 meters (23 feet). I was

My body was in shock from training differently and being broken down so it could be rebuilt.

routinely jumping 7.46 meters (24 feet 6 inches). That's a good jump for a high schooler. But putting on all that weight made it difficult to jump even 7 meters. I had lost almost half a meter or a foot and a half. I talked with Kevin about it.

"It'll be all right," he said. "Trust the plan. Trust the training."

I wanted to believe him, but at the same time I was panicking—so much so that eventually I took my training regimen into my own hands.

The other major problem was that my schedule was out of control. I wasn't getting rest, and I wasn't focused. I was depleted of energy because I wasn't managing myself at all. I was staying up until two or three o'clock in the morning, waking up for a 7:30 class, then tearing my body down at practice. I began to feel it after a couple of weeks, getting fatigued and sick, but I didn't make many changes. I went to bed a little earlier, just enough to stave off exhaustion. And I certainly didn't stop partying.

We had meets almost every weekend, starting in February. We did very few decathlons because they are so hard on the body. Even professional decathletes usually do only three or four a year. Instead, we would do certain events at each meet, maybe the 100, long jump, and shot one week, then running the 400 and throwing the discus the next. As with training, the idea was to work on different events in different competitions.

In the spring of my freshman year, right in the middle of track season, I made a secret decision: I stopped lifting weights. I was freaking out about my bad times and bad marks and thought if I lost weight, I might get back to my high school personal bests. My coaches weren't in the weight room with us, so they had no idea that I had quit. Usually the athletes kept each other accountable, but by this part of the season, we were looser about it. I could wave off going to the weight room, and nobody seemed to notice. It was up to me if I wanted to stick with the program.

The choice got in the way of the cumulative benefit I could have built up. The first year is tough for a decathlete; the second year is even tougher. But in the third year, when your body catches up, everything starts to work for you. It just takes a long time. You are going through changes of routine, in your body, and in training, not to mention the life changes that come with being a college freshman and learning to handle life on your own. I broke under the pressure and made a change to my regimen that I should not have made. My belief in the system faltered.

I dropped back down to about 170 pounds and started doing better right away. I went to the NAIA Indoor National Championships, did the pentathlon (five events: 80-meter hurdles, shot put, high jump, long jump, and 200-meter run) and did okay, but nothing great by my standards. I got a few All-Americans. Then at the NAIA Outdoor National Championships in Florida, I didn't do very well. I did get a good look at athletes who were better than I was, and seeing them kept me from thinking too highly of myself. I realized I might be one of the best freshmen on my team, but there were plenty of superior college athletes. I couldn't get too bigheaded when I flat-out lost.

Because I was still young enough to meet the age requirements, I qualified for the USA Track & Field Junior Nationals, the only one from our team to do so. It wasn't a surprise to anyone that I qualified. In fact, it was kind of expected. Kevin went with me to Denton, Texas, for the meet. I didn't know what to expect. I had only done three college decathlons before then. The first one was at the beautiful Point Loma Nazarene University, where I didn't even break 7,000 points. To make it worse, when I saw where Point Loma was located, right on a cliff overlooking the ocean, I couldn't help thinking, *What was I thinking, going to APU?* I saw kids coming up from the beach in their wet suits and carrying surfboards. I was bitter for a day or two.

The only other "decs" I had done were at the Mount San Antonio College (Mt. SAC) Relays, a big meet in Southern California, and the NAIA Outdoor Nationals. So I had little experience to go on. To my surprise, I won Junior Nationals with 7,312 points, recording the sixth highest U.S. Junior score in history. The second place score was 7,097, and third place was just 6,604. That opened the door for me to compete at the Pan American Junior Athletics Championships, which alternates years with the Junior Olympics. I went to Florida in July for my first international competition and expected to get stomped by some crazy-good athlete from another country. But to my further surprise I won again with a score of 7,207.

Winning at the big meets that summer made me very happy. I had competed against kids who had been doing the dec longer and had impressive marks in individual events, but somehow I had bested them in the overall competition. That summer I stayed at APU and trained with Kevin. I was still spooked about lifting, so I avoided the weight room. As I reflected on my freshman year, I had to think it was good. I was having fun and felt carefree. My parents weren't paying for school. I wasn't fighting anymore, though I was always ready if an opportunity presented itself.

Summer ended, and when everyone came back at the beginning of the semester, there was no celebration over what I had done at Junior Nationals and the Junior Pan Ams. I didn't expect any. A lot of guys didn't even know that I had won those meets, and if they knew, they didn't care. Considering that we had guys training to go to the USA Outdoor Track & Field Championships and the 2000 Olympic Trials, my achievements were fairly minor. I was only scoring 7,300 points, and they were scoring 8,000. I got a couple of pats on the back, and then nobody thought about it anymore.

I expected to do better my sophomore year, and I started to trust Kevin's system more. Little did I know that soon my life would be shattered, and I would find myself in a situation that forever changed me athletically, personally, and spiritually.

FIVE
GOD FIRST!

Outside Engstrom Hall, some friends and I were hanging around one day during my freshman year when a girl from the track team walked by on her way to practice.

"See, she's the type of girl I think I could marry," I said to my buddies. "Someone like that. I like everything about her. Her attitude, her personality—she's a sweet girl."

Her name was Sarah. She was a javelin thrower, and though we had never really talked before, I had seen her around the track. I had even held her hand during team prayer before practice one time. That was the extent of our contact. She seemed to have no interest in me at first. But over time we started talking and got to know each other, and though we were very different people, our personalities clicked. We started casually dating, and in a short time we had a routine of hitting the movie theater after practice. We must have seen every movie that came into the multiplex, including cartoons.

Sarah's upbringing was vastly different from mine. I always joke that she came from a *Leave It to Beaver*–type family. She never got into trouble and was spanked literally one time. That was the extent of her childhood trauma.

I liked everything about Sarah, and soon I began to open up about my life and my goals: I wanted to be a great athlete and maybe even go to the Olympics, I told her. After I did that, I wanted to help kids somehow. My motivation in sharing these dreams was twofold. I knew that if I opened up and let her see my sensitive side, she would like me more. But it wasn't all an act; part of me longed to follow Christ and have the peace I knew He could give me. That side of me naturally emerged when I was with Sarah. She brought out my best aspirations. I knew I could share my feelings and fears with her and not be judged. Soon we were falling in love.

But after sharing all these deep and hopeful things with her when we were alone, I would hang out with my friends and resume my other life. For me, things were good. I was still partying and was on everyone's short list to call when they were throwing a bash. I had everything a college guy could want: a girlfriend, my track scholarship, and my faith when I needed it. What else was there?

My partying upset Sarah, and we started having regular arguments over it.

"You shouldn't be doing this stuff," she would say.

"Where does it say in the Bible that you can't drink?" I would counter. I always looked for the moral gray area to justify what I was doing.

Sarah was much more spiritually mature than I was, and soon I had this nagging feeling that we were unequally yoked—and that I was the "bad" one in the pair. The churches I attended in my youth had driven home the idea that you shouldn't be unequally yoked. When I dated someone in high school, my mom's first question was always, "Is she a Christian? If not, you can't date her. God says not to be unequally yoked." The concept didn't make any sense to me—until I was dating Sarah. Her behavior and lifestyle were so much different from mine. But she had fallen in love with the Bryan I had portrayed to her in private—the caring, future-oriented, softhearted man of God. That wasn't the Bryan I was at the time, though deep down it was who I wanted to be.

Over time I started to have a bad influence on her. She wanted to be part of my world, so she came over to hang out with me and my friends. Little by little she started to compromise her standards. Then she realized what was happening and broke up with me. Soon we got into a cycle of breaking up and getting back together that went on for more than a year.

In the meantime my behavior was getting worse, and I was partying more. Sarah, ironically, became my resident adviser in my sophomore year. I would party and then lie to her about it. On Saturday night my friends would drag me home from someone's house, and I would throw up all over the floor. The next morning I would have a hangover, and she would come over and say, "Hey, what did you do last night?" "Oh, nothing," I would lie. "Stayed home." Then she would find out what I had actually done, and we would fight about it.

Sometimes she would turn a blind eye when, as my RA, she could have disciplined me. It put her in a terrible position. Sometimes it seemed as if we were just too different to ever make it work. She had fallen in love with a guy who claimed to have high aspirations and dreams but was showing little evidence of actually carrying them out.

Olympic Prophecy

My mom kept calling and telling me that she was praying for me, and that I was going to go to the Olympics and win the gold medal. I kept blowing her off because it wasn't a subject I enjoyed talking about. It brought up fears of failure and reminded me of a standard of excellence I thought I would never meet. There was nothing to indicate that what God had "told" her might be true. I was a decent college athlete but nothing more.

I kept plugging away, trying to get better but mainly using the sport to keep myself riding high socially. Kevin and I had set some performance goals, but I was more interested in having fun. Track was important because it paid my way through school and kept me popular. But a true love of the sport wasn't there.

In my sophomore year my body and mind were a little more prepared for the training. I started lifting again and put on more weight, surging from 170 to 180 pounds. But predictably it had the same result: I felt heavy, and my marks worsened. Just before the big Mt. SAC Relays in April, the whole team started to taper on our weight lifting, so I quietly dropped it altogether as I had done my freshman year. I was panicking again and wondering why I wasn't even reaching the personal bests I had hit in high school. Part of me still wanted to prove to everyone that I was worth the full-ride scholarship and that my talk of Olympic dreams wasn't just a bunch of hot air.

> My mom kept calling and telling me that she was praying for me, and that I was going to go to the Olympics and win the gold medal.

I didn't have a lot going for me other than track. It was time to put up or shut up. And I still hated losing. Much of my training was to ensure that I didn't have to experience that feeling very often.

Going to the Olympics was still not a realistic dream, in my assessment. I'd had some success but not nearly the kind of success that I would need to make it to the

Olympic Trials. There was still a 1,000-point gulf between what I was scoring and what I needed to score. I never talked to anyone about my doubts except Sarah. I wasn't going to be that real with anyone else. I just played the role and said, "Yeah, I can make the Olympics."

But my decathlon scores had plateaued. I had improved in some individual events, running a little faster in the 100 and the 110 hurdles, throwing the shot a little farther, going a little higher in the pole vault. I had yet to put it all together into a strong decathlon performance. And in some events I couldn't imagine improving as much as I would need to. Throwing a shot put 16 meters (52 feet 6 inches) when I was presently throwing it 12 meters was as big a goal as making the Olympics. It didn't seem possible.

My body size, too, was a limiting factor. I remember thinking as a freshman: *I'll never be able to bench 315 pounds. My body frame will never be able to handle it. My bones will break.* I was benching a maximum of 275 at the time. Everything pointed to the fact that I was naturally limited in how far I could go.

I didn't do myself any favors with my behavior off the track. I kept crazy hours, getting half the sleep I needed. One time during my sophomore year I actually passed out from exhaustion while walking down the stairs in one of the big classrooms. I fell and hit my head, then woke up and acted as if it was no big deal. But I took it seriously enough that I started going to bed an hour or two earlier.

The urge to party remained. One weekend several of us from the team went to Las Vegas and got trashed. We drove back and made Monday practice that afternoon. We were terribly hungover and threw up in the bushes between runs. Our code of honor said there was no excuse for not showing up and performing even if our performance was subpar. We never missed practice for anything, especially something like that. We would have caught flak from the coaches and the other guys had they known what we had done and the shape we were in.

One Monday Kevin called me into his office for a chat. I was nervous because I had gotten really wasted the weekend before.

"So what did you do this weekend?" he asked lightly.

"Oh, nothing. Just hung out," I said.

"Is that so? That's not what I heard," he said.

He told me what he knew. It was exactly the truth. I couldn't help thinking, *How did he find out? Who told him?*

He finished with a firm, "Do not let it happen again, or there will be consequences."

"Okay," I said, but his warning didn't come close to stopping me. I would have to be more careful about choosing the people I trusted. I was never openly disrespectful to Kevin or my other coaches, and I busted my rear end on the track every day. But I wasn't going to allow them to stand in the way of my having fun. I didn't care who I hurt or disappointed in that pursuit.

I did well in NAIA competition my sophomore year and also competed against athletes from Division I schools. I wasn't dominating the field, but I was doing enough to keep my lifestyle afloat. At the NAIA Outdoor Nationals I won the dec, and I was an All-American in the indoor heptathlon, a seven-event competition. It always felt good to win.

That summer I got hurt and couldn't compete. I lived in campus housing with my friend Jesse, a shot-putter who was hurt too. I got a job at the cafeteria, washing dishes, but I only went when I needed spending money. Jesse and I also worked together at a fireworks stand in a grocery store parking lot. We barbecued every night, hauled a couch outside, and watched TV on our porch, splitting a thirty-pack of beer between us. We played Wiffle ball and spent hours mastering Super Nintendo Track & Field, to the point that we held some online records and had to create a training schedule to keep our hands from being constantly fatigued.

I had no bills to pay, no training to do, no real responsibilities other than working occasionally to supply our beer habit. It seemed to be one of the great summers of my life, but events were closing in on me, and things were about to go off a cliff.

Devastation

Sarah had broken up with me—again—at the end of my sophomore year. I didn't take it too seriously because we always got back together. And when she came back to Southern California from Seattle to attend a mutual friend's wedding during Jesse's and my summer of leisure, we got to talking and dancing and rekindled the relationship. But before she left, she assured me our relationship was off. It was faint assurance, and I knew that when school started, we'd be on again.

During that summer in Seattle, however, Sarah made up her mind that I was a bad influence. This time it wasn't a halfhearted decision—it was for real.

When Sarah came back to campus, she made no contact with me whatsoever. I was stunned. Suddenly I realized she might be serious about breaking up for good. I kept my cool and tried to talk to her and get her to come back around. She wouldn't return my increasingly desperate-sounding messages.

Then to my horror I found out she was going on group dates and seeing other guys. I frantically researched her new social habits, talking to mutual friends and gathering all the information I could. For the first time it seemed that our relationship really was in free fall, that she didn't care about me, and that I might lose her forever if I didn't do something quickly.

I panicked. For all that I had put her through, I still thought she was the girl I could marry. I began to have self-recriminating conversations with myself. *Bryan, you just screwed up something really good*, I told myself. *This was the best thing in your life, and you took it for granted. You'll regret for the rest of your life that you let this happen.* I sank into a complete malaise.

I sat in my nearly bare apartment, furnished with only a phone in the middle of the room, a television sitting on a box against the wall, and my sleeping bag on the floor because school had not officially started yet and we did not bother to decorate. My roommates invited me to go out with them, but I uncharacteristically turned them down. I felt literal heartache for the first time in my life, and I couldn't get it to stop. I was so depressed that I felt nauseous. I was lost inside myself, and I started to pray like I never had before.

"God, if You just let her call, I'll change everything about my life," I said one day as I was looking at the phone. Miraculously the phone rang, and it was Sarah. Hallelujah!

"Your roommates told me you haven't been eating," she said, without much feeling. "Let me pick you up and take you out for lunch."

I couldn't believe my good fortune. As I got ready to go, I made God all sorts of pledges to follow through on my promise of a changed life.

Sarah picked me up (she had a car; I didn't) and took me to a sandwich shop on Route 66 near APU. We pulled in and parked in front. She opened the door and started to get out of the car, but I just sat there. I was still so brokenhearted that I couldn't even move. I needed answers about our future before I could do anything else.

"I'm not hungry," I said.

She closed the door and asked, "What's going on?"

"Are we ever going to get back together?" I asked her point-blank.

She looked at me and said, "We'll never get back together until you become the man of God that I know you want to be and that I know He wants you to be."

Her choice of words made me instantly angry. *Wow, the nerve of this person!* I thought. *Typical Christian girl, using God as a cop-out.* I felt like telling her, "Don't mess around with me. If you don't like me, tell me so I can cut bait and be done with it. But don't sit here and give me the Christian answers like, 'I feel like God is saying we shouldn't be together anymore.' Or 'I need to concentrate on my relationship with God.'" Thoughts were sprinting through my mind, but I could hardly focus on any of them. I was trying to figure out a way to trap her into giving me an actual answer. I wanted to force her to admit her feelings, or lack of feelings, for me.

I finally settled on a semitheological approach. Knowing that being a Christian was a personal decision and that nobody could truly know whether you had made that decision, I cleverly asked her, "So how will you know when I make that decision? How could you possibly know that I have decided to turn my life around and live for Christ?" I thought that I had cornered her and that she was going to have to give me a straight answer. I thought she would have to admit that she was using "God talk" as a cover for some other motive.

Instead she said simply, "I'll know."

What do you mean, "I'll know"? I thought, steaming. I hated the vagueness of this statement. I am goal oriented and always want to know how to achieve my next objective. If you give me a goal,

> "We'll never get back together until you become the man of God that I know you want to be and that I know He wants you to be."

I'm going to reach it. That's how I operate. I wanted her to tell me specifically what to do so we could get back together, and then everything would be okay.

But I didn't get the answer I wanted, and we never made it inside the sandwich shop. She ended up taking me back to my apartment, and we parted on neutral terms more or less. She went back to ignoring me—and it wasn't that she was just playing hard to get. She seemed to be starting a new life entirely without me. That scared me, and I desperately tried to figure out a plan of action for winning her back.

For the first time I critically considered my lifestyle. I had always known right from wrong, but I had never seen much harm in what I was doing. Having my relationship with Sarah on the line made the damaging effects of my choices more real than ever. It wasn't my mom, dad, stepdad, teacher, principal, professor, or coach telling me I needed to change. It was my own heart.

As I was thinking it all through, the idea popped into my head: *What would people say about me if I wasn't in the room? Say I had died or just turned around and walked out. What would they say about me?* The only thing I could come up with, even for people who were my friends, was, "Oh, yeah, I know Bryan. He's a really good athlete."

But even that wasn't true. I was a thousand points away from a national-level score—an insane amount. So the pride I took in being a good athlete was not well founded. It was a smoke screen.

> The pride I took in being a good athlete was not well founded. It was a smoke screen.

I felt devastated by this judgment of myself. It was plain to me that in spite of my social status on campus, I was worthless. I was all bluff. There was nothing to me, certainly nothing worth emulating. Sarah was right to leave me.

At a loss for how to change and how to discover a part of me that might be worth building on, I began doing the only thing that I could think of: I woke up earlier than usual, went to the cafeteria, and read my Bible. I wasn't doing it for show; I was doing it because I needed answers and I was willing to do anything to get them. I wanted to see if the Bible and the Christian life would really offer me anything or if it would be just another dead-end road on my search for self-worth.

Day after day I sat by myself with my breakfast to one side and my Bible open before me, reading about Jesus' disciples. I was intrigued by the question of what it meant to be a disciple of Christ. As I studied the behavior of the disciples, I concluded that their core characteristic was a desire to be molded into the image of Jesus. They learned how to be Christlike from watching Him day after day. Applying that idea to my life, I began to think, *Who is someone I want to be like? Who can disciple me or mentor me?* If I was going to change, I wanted a real, live model, somebody who was doing his best to be Christlike in everyday life.

I thought about it for a while and tried to identify some candidates. I posed my original question this way: What did people say about some of the people I knew when they left the room?

Coach Mike Barnett was my throws coach and the head coach for women's track and field at APU. Coach Barnett, an APU alum, was a javelin thrower who had placed seventh in the Barcelona games, which is still the highest finish in that event for an American. When he left the room, people said, "It's amazing how that guy always puts family first." That's what stood out about Coach Barnett. He had traveled with me and coached me the year I went to the Junior Pan Ams, and I had watched him grow as a coach in the couple of years since then. He always did what he thought was right, even if it meant apologizing and admitting he was wrong. I hadn't seen a lot of guys do that. He was humble and straightforward while still being confident.

Then there was Kevin. When Kevin left the room, people talked about what an encourager he was, how he knew how to get people to do things that sometimes they didn't believe they could do. Kevin was our leader. We were having weekly Bible studies at his house as a team, and he led worship on his guitar, sometimes even in tune. He showed me that you could be a Christian and have fun. He also showed me a lot of grace as a coach. There were probably times he should have kicked me off the team, but he chose to stick with me.

I thought seriously about asking Kevin or Coach Barnett to be my mentor, but my relationship was too close with both of them. It would have been tough to maintain a coach-athlete relationship and also a mentor-protégé relationship. I had to find someone else.

Then I thought of Terry Franson, the dean of students at APU. What did people say about Terry when he left the room? Only good things: they talked about how much integrity he had, how humble he was, how family was so important to him. Terry had been a coach for many years and won a bunch of NAIA national championships for APU in track and field. He was named NAIA Coach of the Year ten years in a row, and he had coached Olympic athletes in 1984, 1988, and 1992. He left coaching to get into administration and, at the time, was suffering with a vocal problem that kept him from talking louder than a whisper. The way he had gone through his struggle and the way he led his life were exemplary.

There's my mentor, I thought.

D-group

I made an appointment with Terry at the school coffee shop and unloaded on him a little bit about my personal problems.

"Coach Franson, life has been tough," I finally said. "I feel like I need to have a mentor. I was wondering if you have the time to mentor me."

He said he was honored that I would ask him and then told me,

"Let me go home and pray about this. I'll get back to you in a day or two."

A day or so later he called and said, "Bryan, I'd love to take you on and mentor you. But my schedule is very busy. If I could get you to join this group of students I meet with on Tuesday mornings, that would work best for me. It's a discipleship group that gets together for breakfast, and we talk about life, what we're struggling with, and the good things that are happening. It's not always a deep discussion. You may have gotten an A on a test, or you're going to see your parents this weekend. We just share life together. But I need to ask them first. And if you become part of the group, you need to understand that this is a commitment. If we are going to commit to you, you need to commit to us. There's no missing D-group."

I was more than ready to try it, and I told him so. He brought up the idea with the guys in the group, and they generously let me join them. They even changed the day of the week on which they met to accommodate my schedule. Soon I was getting up earlier than I had ever wanted to so I could meet with guys I didn't know to talk about things I had never spent a lot of time talking about before.

There were four or five of us, plus Terry, and the members changed year by year as people graduated or moved on. It was a big step for me to suddenly be in an intimate setting with people I didn't know. I had always been a sports guy, always hanging around with the track team. I knew virtually nobody outside the athletics program. And to make it more awkward, I felt that I had nothing in common with the other guys in the group. One of them was into theater and making films. Another played rugby for an intramural league but was never going to do anything in the sport professionally. Another was into music. None of it was part of my world. What could we have in common?

In the following weeks I saw that the group was exactly what

Terry said it was: guys doing nothing more than sharing life as you would if you went out to coffee with friends. We talked about classes, about work, about whatever was important to us. Once in a while someone would be struggling with something, and we'd all give input. Sometimes Terry brought a card with a verse or thought for the week that we would discuss. It was always open and flowing. It was a safe place where we could talk. And nobody missed the meetings.

As I met with these guys and as other parts of my life began to change, something unexpected happened. Sarah caught wind of it and started talking to me again. She noticed that I was going to bed earlier and starting to have a reasonable daily routine. She saw that I was setting priorities and even going to church and chapel. Slowly she started letting me back into her life.

After a while it became apparent that we might start a relationship again, but Sarah set new ground rules. "If we're going to do this again, we're going to start from a clean state," she said. "No more compromises, no more mistakes." She took this so seriously that she insisted we not talk for a while and that I think of a creative way to ask her out again, as if it were the first time. I did that, and on our "first" date we didn't even hold hands. Everything was brand-new.

For the first time in a long time, I had hope. Hope that maybe living clean would work. Hope that God actually did hear and answer prayers. Hope that maybe Sarah and I had a future together.

Then, in one instant, it all fell apart.

Rock Bottom

I was competing in a track meet at APU and unexpectedly, in between events, I saw a girl from my past standing around. I had not seen her in a long time, and we had never dated, but we had fooled around a little bit. Things had ended badly, and I really didn't want to see her, especially in the middle of the meet and more especially because things were going so well with Sarah. I had changed my life and was walking a different path, so when she started coming closer, I thought, *Great. This is the last person I want to talk to.* I ignored her as long as I could and kept doing my events. But finally she approached me directly and said, "I need to talk to you."

"Yeah, what?" I said. "I'm in the middle of a meet."

"We've got a problem," she said.

"What do you mean, 'We've got a problem'?" I asked.

"I've got an STD," she said flatly.

I was stunned.

"Okay," I said. "What does that have to do with me?"

She explained that though we hadn't had sex, we had done some things that might have exposed me to the disease.

"I think you'd better get checked out," she concluded and walked away.

My world was shattered. I was so blindsided by the news that I could hardly finish the meet. It had happened so quickly that it seemed unreal. I kept doing my events but couldn't concentrate. Kevin knew something was wrong and asked what was going on. I told him I had just received some distressing news, and he told me to do my best and finish it out. I did, but it wasn't worth anything because my mind was in a million places.

Getting a checkup as soon as possible took precedence over everything else. After I left the meet, I hurried over to the student health clinic, but it was a Friday evening, and the clinic was about to close. The earliest they could take me was on Monday morning.

I went back to my dorm and started frantically researching this particular STD on the Internet. I did not let my roommates or Sarah or anyone else know what was happening—I made some excuse about being worn-out—but I was dying on the inside, and my mind was caught up in a whirlwind of unanswered questions. *Did I have this STD? If so, would I be able to have kids? Would Sarah marry me? Could you pass on the disease to your kids or to your spouse? What were the long-term effects going to be? Could I ever get rid of it?*

It sounds silly now, but I kept thinking that if I did become a successful athlete, would I be one of those who had a very public and embarrassing problem? Would I be the guy doing TV commercials for a treatment for this particular STD?

Everything I wanted in life was in jeopardy. I had recalibrated my desires and goals toward having a family and was finally putting the proper effort into my training as an athlete. Those efforts were already bearing fruit, and I was improving in my events. Now it looked as if my future was out the window, gone, history. Not only would Sarah leave me, but no girl in her proper mind would marry a guy who had an STD. My dreams of being a father and a respectable athlete were gone too.

I spent the weekend in my dorm room, waiting for my appointment with the doctor Monday morning and doing hour after hour of research on the Internet, desperately seeking some glimmer of hope.

I also found myself in a deepening spiritual pit. The more I thought about it, the more unfair it seemed that this would happen now. When my roommates left, I stayed home, pacing the room and cussing God out. "How dare You do this to me now!" I shouted. "I'm reading my Bible. I've got a mentor. I'm going to a discipleship group. Sarah and I are back together. I'm going to church. I'm praying. I'm worshipping You. I rededicated my life to You. I'm doing everything I'm supposed to be doing. How dare You take it all away! How dare You!"

I was so angry that I threw my Bible against the wall. Then I banged my head against the wall—hard. I could not believe this would happen just when everything was going right. I felt as if I was being punished for making all the right choices. I had always heard that when you ask for forgiveness, God throws your sins in the "sea of forgetfulness," and they are gone forever. But instead of wiping my slate clean, He seemed to be holding my past sins against me.

Instead of going to church, I stayed holed up in my room. Then late Sunday night or early Monday morning, I reached a point of utter personal crisis. I was on the verge of saying, "Forget You, God. I don't want anything to do with You if this is how it's going to be." I was close to turning my back on my faith. I sat there at the computer, lost and completely broken. I had been challenging Him all day with my "How dare Yous?"

But I felt Him respond: *No, Bryan, how dare you think that just because you gave your life over to Me, you wouldn't have to face the consequences of choices you made previously?*

That one statement was enough to crush me. I saw the truth in an instant. Would a serial killer go free if he gave his life to Christ in the middle of a trial? No. He would still have to serve his sentence. So I had to face the consequences of foolish choices I had made. I could not believe how self-centered I had been, to think that since I gave my life to Christ, everything would be okay. I felt small and insignificant as I caught a glimpse of how big God is.

I gave up and got down on my knees. I had reached the point of total surrender. I said, "Okay, Lord. If I'm the loneliest person on the planet, if Sarah won't marry me, if I can't have kids, if my friends all leave because I'm starting to follow Christ and I won't party with them anymore, if all I'm known for is being that STD treatment guy—if that's what my future looks like, and it's the worst life I could imagine, the very opposite of everything I want—then I guess it'll just be me and You."

That was my prayer. There was no campfire, no altar call, no preacher. It was just me alone in a dorm room. I didn't say, "Oh, Lord, I love You. I'm going to follow You." I simply gave up and said, "Lord, I don't have anybody else. There's no one else I know who will stand with me. I guess I'll take a chance on my faith, and it will just be me and You."

I wish I could say I instantly felt better or had a rush of warm, reassuring feelings that everything would be fine. But the only thing I really felt was the relief of having given up. I didn't have the energy to fight anymore. My future was in God's hands for the first time in my life. I knew it might not mean everything would get better automatically. It might just be me and Him. But I had made a decision that would completely change my life.

And without knowing it, I had taken the most important step toward becoming a champion.

SIX
SUDDEN
SUCCESS

Exhausted, I fell asleep. Monday morning I had the first appointment with the doctor at our school medical center, housed in a modest building not far from the track. I arrived and found it to be a warm, welcoming place. The nurses and receptionist were friendly, but I was painfully aware that they knew why I was there. As comfortable and private and discreet as it all was, I couldn't help imagining them looking over my file and talking about me in another room. Shame clung to me like a sweaty shirt after a workout.

Finally the nurse led me into an exam room, and moments later in shuffled this beloved older physician who was well-known by the students at APU. I am not easily embarrassed, but being in the room with this man and knowing I would probably have to share things I didn't want to share made me feel vulnerable and stupid. Not to mention that APU was a Christian university where this kind of behavior was not exactly condoned.

"Good morning, Bryan," he said as he looked over his clipboard with the nurse's notes.

"Hi, thanks for seeing me," I said. I had strongly conflicting impulses. I wanted to run out of the office and avoid the embarrassing conversation I knew would ensue. I also wanted to lay it all out because I felt my life was literally on the line. I stuck with the latter.

"What can I help you with?" he asked, taking a seat on his rolling stool.

I took a deep breath.

"A girl just told me she has an STD, and I think I may have it."

"Okay, which one?" he asked matter-of-factly.

I told him.

He nodded. "Why do you think you may have it? Have you had intercourse with her?" he asked.

This guy doesn't waste any time, I thought.

"No," I said.

"Why don't you explain to me what you and this girl did?" he said.

Here we go, I thought. I began stumbling through the embarrassing facts, blushing and speaking softly, as if my shame could be lessened at lower volume.

He took it in clinically. "How long ago was this?" he asked.

"Nine or ten months ago."

"Have you had any symptoms?"

"No."

At that point I thought I saw him smirk.

"I think it's safe to say you're fine."

Fine? I thought. *It can't be that easy.*

"Are you sure?" I asked.

"Yes," he said. "I would be very surprised if you contracted her STD, given the contact you described. And the incubation period is six months. If you haven't had symptoms by now, you're in the clear."

He stood up, smiled, and got ready to step out. I felt like hugging him. The relief now cascading over me was greater than any I had ever felt. My entire life had been handed back to me. I shook his hand, thanked him a couple of times, and walked out behind him.

Outside, the campus seemed alive with color, sound, and sweet smells. Everything had changed. I stood there smiling a big goofy grin, not caring who saw me. I didn't care about being cool. I didn't care if I looked crazy. I was free! The sunlight felt different. The trees and grass and sky looked more vibrant than ever. Everything in the world had come back to life—and so had I. I felt like someone walking out of a dark prison cell. "Thank You, God," I said under my breath. "Thank You so much."

Then, as I began to walk home, another thought suddenly intruded: *Bryan, you just dodged a bullet. You went through all that for nothing. It was just a scare. The fear wasn't real. Look at you now—you're in the clear! Go back to what you were doing. It's time to party.*

I considered it for a moment. If I wanted to, I could go back to partying and just be more careful. I could finish out my college career in style. The thought was attractive for a moment. I imagined what that life would look like and where that course would take me. It offered what seemed like innocent fun, but now I knew it also offered heartache and destruction of my body, my morals, my emotions, my spirit. It would be reckless and dangerous to go back, and maybe next time I wouldn't get away with it. Without any fanfare as I walked across the APU campus, I closed the door forever on the old lifestyle. *I'm done with that*, I thought. *This is my moment. I'm making a change.*

The vision of the destructive path had been too strong.

Looking back, I think God wanted to take the commitment I had made in the aftermath of losing Sarah and brand it into my heart.

My decision to follow Christ had not been life changing; it had been a means to an end—a way to get Sarah back and to experience some of the benefits of the Christian life, such as peace and joy. I could have easily walked away from it. I was reading my Bible and going to church, but I was still running the show. I was following God on my terms. He wanted me to follow Him on His terms.

When I hit bottom and realized how helpless I was, I didn't just commit—I surrendered to Christ. I gave up entirely and became wholeheartedly His.

Transitioning

From that moment on my life completely changed. Sometimes it almost sounds like a fairy tale because the transition was so sudden. I was now running as fast as I could *away* from the harmful things I had been involved in, and I was running *to* God for everything I needed. I was not outspoken about it. I kept my head down and did my own thing. But inside, a revolution had taken place. For the first time I was doing what my mom and APU had been trying to tell me to do for years: putting God first.

Sarah noticed the change before anyone else did. She could see it was a change of heart, not just of convenience. We had been in a trial period, but we decided to make it official that we were dating again.

My relationships with certain friends started to go bad. There were some guys whom, I'm ashamed to say, I had influenced and even bullied into partying with me. Now I was rejecting the lifestyle I had always promoted, and they didn't understand why. They thought it was because of Sarah, and they resented it. I hadn't shared with them or anyone what had happened with my scare and my visit to the doctor. I tried to tell them, "I've changed. I cannot keep going the way I was going." But they didn't buy it.

For a while they waited for it to blow over. They thought I would snap out of it and revert to my old self. But I didn't. I became even more interested in the things of God, more interested in going to church, more determined to live right. After a while they stopped inviting me to parties. To make it worse, some of these guys were my roommates, and soon we stopped talking. We just passed right by without saying a word. I spent more time alone and at Sarah's house.

Often I heard my old friends talk about their weekend activities and their parties, how crazy and out of control everybody was. For a second I missed that feeling of having no cares, no worries. But then the truth smacked me in the face. Partying is anything but carefree. You have to worry about your health, about looking cool to everyone, about the consequences of your actions the next morning. After a while I couldn't remember what was fun about getting so drunk that I couldn't walk and waking up the next morning feeling horrible and disgusting—headaches, nausea, throwing up. I must have been crazy to think that was a good time.

I enjoyed the comparatively simple life I began to lead. One fear I had expressed during my heart-to-heart with God was that if I followed Him, I would be lonely. It would mean hanging out at church on the weekends and having boring friends. What I found instead was that living clean and having a pure heart were much more fun than wrecking my life every weekend. And the new relationships spurred me to my best, not my worst.

In the next few months I became more grounded than I had ever been. I continued to meet with my D-group, and those early morning meetings shaped my life. It wasn't just the Bible study and the conversations we had about life and spiritual things. It was the simple fact of being there without fail. The friendship of those guys meant the world to me.

Through my D-group God was teaching me what commitment

looked like. It meant showing up no matter what and no matter how I felt that early in the morning. Soon I began to ask myself, *How do I show God the same level of commitment I show to this group? How do I really put God first and make it more than a motto? What does it mean to be a sold-out follower of Christ?* I would ask people, "How do I know what my priorities are? How do I know I'm putting God first?"

A couple of them suggested that whatever I spent the most time doing was my top priority. That worried me because I spent the largest chunk of my time at the track. If I trained for five, six, or seven hours a day, did that mean I had to pray and read my Bible more than that? How did I keep God number one in my life and track number two or three?

It may sound like a simple problem to solve, but I was serious about putting God first. I didn't want to blow it.

Over the next few months, through much thought and many conversations and internal debates, I concluded that if everything I did was Christ focused, I didn't need to spend hours praying and doing devotions to please Him. Rather, I needed to have a Christ-centered perspective on everything I did and keep Him consciously in mind as I went through my day.

As a result my perspective on track began to change. Instead of wanting to succeed so I could be famous and have lots of money, I began to look on it as a tool that God might someday use. I realized how limited and immature my view of my gift had been up to that point. Slowly but surely training became a form of meditation, of honoring Him—of worship. Day by day I gave it all back to Christ so He could use it for something beyond me.

Understanding commitment also helped me to understand what love really is. I had often said that I loved track. But now I wondered what that really meant. That it made me happy? That it met my needs? What was love? A warm, fuzzy feeling? A transaction of some sort? What did it mean that I loved God or Sarah or my family? The question consumed me.

My previous concept of love was pretty shallow. I thought when you loved a woman, either you had a physical relationship with her, or you bought her gifts. Love was a feeling, an attraction, and it could go away. It was the same with track. I loved track when it was serving my needs or when it made me feel good. But I didn't love it when I had to get up early to work out. My definition of love didn't carry me too far.

If love was a feeling, then nothing was stable. It could come and go like the wind. And if love was a feeling, then God's love toward us was based on convenience and whim too. I knew that wasn't true.

The more I investigated what love is, by reading the Bible and talking with others, the more I realized that love is actually commitment—a choice. I turned to 1 Corinthians 13 (NKJV): Love "hopes all things, endures all things" (v. 7), and "Love never fails" (v. 8). The idea rocked my world. It was not a feeling, though it could involve feelings. It was something much deeper and solid. To say I loved something or someone meant I would choose that thing or that person even when I didn't feel like it. If I loved track, I would choose it on the days it was easy and on the days it was hard. If I loved Sarah, I would choose her even when the feelings of romance and joy weren't there.

Love became something not passive and emotional—something that happened to me—but something I could control. This solved an old problem: I could not relate to the idea that God loves me and I should love Him back because I thought it was something I had to feel. And I didn't always feel love for God. But now it was in my power to love Him 100 percent of the time. I could love God, Sarah, my family, or track by choosing to, no matter what I happened to be feeling.

Love suddenly made the important things in my life seem priceless. It was priceless to me that Sarah would choose me even though someone was probably out there who could give her a better life than I could. Out of everyone in the world, she handpicked me and closed the door on everyone else. That was love. It was priceless to me that God would choose me even when I had been so bad to Him and to other people. That was His love. There was certainly someone who deserved the blessings more than I did.

Love made me take track more seriously because I was choosing it now. I was giving it my commitment even when I did not feel like it. It was probably the biggest spiritual lesson that I had ever learned and one that continues to shape my life.

Not only was I learning big spiritual lessons, but school was going better than ever too. My grades came up seemingly on their own. I can't say I was enjoying school any more than I had because I was never a classroom guy. But I found myself growing personally in unexpected ways because of my major studies in social work. I learned things about myself in those classes that helped me put into context both what I had been through as a child and the choices I had made as a result. It was empowering to realize that I was not alone, that there was a body of research about people just like me. Much of the bitterness I held, unfairly, against other people drained away, and I felt a process of healing begin. I was growing and changing and maturing as never before.

Results on the Track

This personal and spiritual growth had an unexpected result: I began to improve dramatically as an athlete.

After Christmas break I came back to school from Hawaii and started competing for the indoor season. I was so wrapped up in what was happening in my nonathletic life that I didn't pay much attention to my scores. Track was a big thing in my life, but now God was bigger, and so was my relationship with Sarah.

I had won the NAIA decathlon and pentathlon titles in 2000, and in 2001 I won the NAIA Indoor Nationals again. In March 2001 I competed in a dec at Point Loma Nazarene University and got second place with a score of 7,099, well short of my best score of 7,373, which I had set the year before. The next meet was the huge Mt. SAC (San Antonio College) Relays, held on both the Mt. SAC and APU campuses—a major meet on the West Coast, drawing athletes and teams from out of state. It employs a waterfall start, which means that multiple events take place at the same time on different parts of the track. That is nice for the athletes because you go from one event to another without a lot of time in between.

I felt incredibly relaxed going into it. In the past I had made the mistake of "chasing my marks," as Kevin put it, trying too hard to force what comes naturally. That mind-set kicked in especially when I did poorly in one event. The temptation was to go out and try harder on the next one, but that only threw me out of rhythm.

Part of competing at a high level is learning how to relax in the midst of intense competition, and I felt relaxed at Mt. SAC for two reasons. First, I had already concluded that I wasn't a top-level athlete and really didn't have a chance to do well at Mt. SAC. Yes, I was good in the NAIA and had won a few national championships, but I hadn't really accomplished anything beyond that. I was nowhere near the professional guys competing nationally. I wasn't at a Division I school or winning NCAA championships. I was just a guy with some raw talent competing at a small Christian university in Southern California.

Second, my focus was no longer primarily on track; it was on God and my relationship with Sarah. I was no longer using track to prove my worth to myself and others or to glorify myself. Though I was committed to my sport, track took a backseat now, where it belonged. That took much of the pressure off.

I didn't think much about Mt. SAC until the day it started. I competed just as I did at every other dec. But when I looked up at the board at the end of the second day, I saw a score I never thought I would see next to my name: 7,980 points, a whopping 600-point jump in my personal best.

Suddenly I was at a whole new level. I was twenty-one years old, and I had just qualified for the USA Outdoor Championships. I would be heading to Eugene, Oregon, to compete with the best decathletes in the country.

My coaches were ecstatic. They hugged my neck and congratulated me as I tried to take in the size of the score. I was stunned by what I had done, but Kevin wasn't. He has a habit of talking up his athletes and making each of them seem like Superman in his telling. We usually took that as nothing more than talk. But he knew the potential was there for a big meet. My personal bests in each event were good enough that if I came close to them all in one meet, my score would be around 8,000.

But it's no easy thing to do in a decathlon, and I had never gotten close to posting personal bests in every event before. The dec requires a special ability to go through those ten events, each with very different requirements, and perform consistently close to your best. It does not require you to be your best, but to perform consistently across the range of events. Somehow I had done that at Mt. SAC. I "put one together," as we say in the sport.

> I was no longer using track to prove my worth to myself and others or to glorify myself.

I had shocked those observing, the other athletes, and myself. Nobody expects someone to come into a major competition and post a 600-point improvement over his previous best score. It just doesn't happen. But it happened to me at Mt. SAC.

In the next couple of weeks I competed at the NAIA Outdoor National Championships and won the long jump and a couple of other events. I also won the NAIA Outstanding Performer award, which was a real honor. Then I trained like crazy for the rest of the summer.

Qualifying for the USA Championships is great, but as the reality sunk in, I began to get used to the idea. I learned that lots of athletes qualify. It doesn't mean you are an elite athlete, though it does mean you have the chance to be one. I kept my focus on God and on important relationships and made sure track didn't consume me. I trained all summer and was often the only one out there. People passing by saw only a guy running the track or practicing the long jump or one of the throws. But in reality I was worshipping God through my sport.

The Big Time

I arrived at the University of Oregon in Eugene for the championships and was probably the youngest guy there. I was wide-eyed; I had never competed in an event even close to that size. Kevin was an invaluable resource, having been to the USA Championships with Dave Johnson and a few other decathletes. Every step of the way he told me how to manage the experience. We stayed in a hotel on the river and had a surprisingly relaxed run-up to the meet. We prayed together about the competition and spent a lot of time in the hotel pool and sauna, just having a good time. We continued a tradition we started in 1998, when I qualified for Junior Nationals, of eating at Outback Steakhouse the night before the meet. I always had the salmon.

On day one I was all nerves, and Kevin had to force me to eat breakfast. As usual those nerves went away when I hit the track and got into the rhythm of competition. Kevin and I prayed together before the meet, something we have done ever since. I put together some good marks, then went back to the hotel and relaxed.

On day two I put together good marks as well. The stadium was big and the energy and excitement electric, but I kept my focus on each event. Many of the other athletes were amped up and feeling the pressure. I could hear urgent conversations between them and their coaches. I could hear them yell at themselves during or after an event. For my part I felt more grounded than ever before, not in my performance but in Christ. I had nothing to lose. I hadn't expected to be here. This was all a bonus. Kevin wasn't uptight about anything. He put no pressure on me. I felt calm in the middle of the storm, and that calmness allowed me to do what I love to do: compete.

During the discus, Kevin was sitting in the stands next to the UCLA throws coach, Art Venegas, who has coached many Olympic and world champions. I didn't throw particularly well that day, but I guess it was good enough to impress Art. "This kid has it," he told Kevin. "He's going to really compete." Then again, maybe he just didn't expect a smaller guy like me to be able to throw well because most of the top throwers look like bodybuilders, and I'm petite by comparison.

After nine events Kevin sat me down at the warm-up field. Kevin never lets me look at the scoreboard during a meet, so at that point I didn't know how I was doing. I just knew I felt good.

"Okay, listen," he said. "You're winning."

I missed the next few sentences because I couldn't believe what he had said.

"I'm winning?" I interrupted, just to be sure.

"Yeah," he said. "You're ahead in points."

"That's crazy," I said.

"It's where we're at," Kevin said. "There are two guys right behind you, Kip Janvrin and Phil McMullen. They're going to run the 1500 fast, maybe in 4:10. They're going to beat you by thirty seconds. You can't make them run any slower, so don't even worry about what they're doing. Just go out and do your best. Try to run it in 4:40, nothing special, and we will hang onto third and make the world championship team."

Janvrin, a member of the 2000 Olympic team and the oldest man (at age thirty-five) ever to compete in the decathlon at the Olympics, was one of the best 1500 runners of all time. He had won the event at the 2000 Olympics. He would go on to set the American record for most career decathlon wins (forty) and most decathlon scores over 8,000 points (twenty-six).

"Okay, listen," he said. "You're winning."

McMullen had been an Olympic alternate for the 2000 Olympics after placing fourth at the Olympic Trials. He was considered one of the top two decathletes in the United States.

Then there was me. The 1500 was, and remains, my weakest event. I haven't found the key to that one yet. At the time I could run it in 4:45. But to run it in 4:40 was asking a lot. I had stopped lifting again and thinned down to about 175, which might help me. Now my head was swimming as I lined up for the final event.

I'm winning USA Championships, I thought, but it didn't seem real. I was just a kid from Hawaii, a guy who had spent the better part of his college years goofing around. How had I gotten here?

Just like that the gun went off, and sure enough, Kip and Phil took off as if they were in a drag race. Soon they were so far ahead that you had to look across the infield just to see them. Runners jockeyed for position on the inside lane. I was deaf to everything but the machinelike breathing of the guys around me and the thundering sound of our shoes on the rubberized track.

I poured every ounce of effort into it, pushing as hard as I could to hold onto a third-place overall finish. When I crossed the finish line, I looked up at the board. Kip and Phil had indeed run an astonishing 4:14.96 and 4:17.04, respectively. But I ran it in 4:38.93, the fastest I have ever run the 1500 to this day. It was good enough for a bronze medal in my first USA Championship competition. I had scored 8,169, the fourth-best total by an American that year, and made my first world championship team. Kevin ran down to the field and gave me a hug.

"You did it," he said.

I still couldn't believe it. I looked up at the big board to make sure my name was up there. It was. Bryan Clay—third place. It was as if my mom's prediction was coming true before my eyes, one step at a time.

I knew that my training was only part of the story and not the most important part. Keeping my priorities in the right order had brought me there. I had stumbled into greater success than I thought possible. My new model was: God first, family second, and track third. Putting God first elevated everything else in my life. I had sold out to Him, and He had given everything back, with greater success.

I was amazed and proud that I had performed so well in Eugene, and as I returned to Southern California, I knew it wouldn't have happened had God not held the top spot in my life.

He was laying the foundation for amazing successes yet to come. But first I would experience humiliating failure.

SEVEN
DISASTER ON THE WORLD STAGE

Every time you move to a higher level in sports, people start to make a sideline game out of downplaying your success and ability. As soon as I took third at the USA Championships, observers of the decathlon pretty much agreed that I was maxed out and that this was the highest I would ever place.

I was inclined to agree with them. The leaders in the sport were scoring 8,800 or 8,900 points. I had scored a mere 8,169. Decathlon scores in the United States were lower than in the past, and I soon concluded that I had placed third because it was a down year. Not only were scores down across the board, but Tom Pappas, the leading American decathlete, didn't compete at the USA Championships that year. *He certainly would have beaten me*, I thought. The critics seemed right—under normal circumstances, I would not have made the U.S. team.

At the same time I allowed myself to harbor small, secret hopes that maybe one day everything would come together for me to make an Olympic team. Back home I plugged numbers into the decathlon calculator and saw that if I hit my best marks, I could score 8,300 points. If I improved just slightly in each one, I could score even higher. Instead of running 10.50, I might be able to run 10.45 in the 100, for instance. Instead of jumping 7.30 meters (24 feet), maybe I could jump 7.40 meters as I had done in high school. That was 10 centimeters (4 inches), a realistic number and not far from what I was doing already. I printed out a set of goals and showed them to Kevin.

"Go for it," he said. "Those are completely reasonable."

My mom's words kept coming back to me: I was destined to become the best in the world. In the back of my mind I gave it a bit more room for consideration. *Maybe during a down year for the United States in decathlon, if I get a little better and get a little lucky, I can score high enough to squeak into a spot on the Olympic team*, I thought.

At the same time I am a pretty realistic guy, and I thought it was unlikely to happen, so I did not spend a lot of serious time on it. It was a distant dream that resided deep in my heart—and in my mother's prayers.

I did not have much time to consider questions about my future. I had made my first world championship team—before even graduating from college—and a few weeks after my surprise showing in Eugene, I flew to Edmonton, Alberta, Canada, for the World Outdoor Championships. Kevin traveled with me, and Mom flew in from Hawaii to be there, which was exciting for me.

But it was to be a disaster.

Unnerved

From the beginning of Worlds, everything was new and different. It was the first time I had to wake up early for a meet: 5:00 a.m. to be at the track by 7:00 a.m. for a groggy warm-up. From the moment

I arrived I was surrounded by the greatest decathletes in the world, people I had read about in magazines or seen on TV, guys with towering scores and legendary individual marks, many of which I knew by heart. As I tried to warm up, I went from being distracted to being terrified by their presence. Everywhere I turned was another famous athlete. I barely completed a normal warm-up.

At 8:00 a.m. they herded us into the call room to check our spikes and uniforms. I had never been through such a process, never been in a call room—and I was soon unnerved. Coaches weren't allowed to go in with us. I didn't know how I fit in with the other athletes. They had never seen me and barely regarded me.

I sat by myself, hoping nobody would notice how nervous I was. Then Roman Sebrle, the best decathlete in the world at the time, sat beside me without so much as glancing in my direction. He had just done what no decathlete had ever done: scored more than 9,000 points—9,026, to be exact. He had also won a silver medal at the Olympics in Sydney.

Tomas Dvorak, a Czech and Roman's training partner, came over and sat on the other side of me, also oblivious to my presence. Tomas had held the previous world record for a few months only to have Roman break it with his otherworldly 9,026. These two guys were the titans of the sport, and they were so close that I could smell them.

Across the room I spotted Estonian Erki Nool, the 2000 Olympic gold medalist. In walked Dean Macey, the charismatic six-foot-five-inch decathlete from Great Britain who, like me, had burst onto the scene at a very young age. Macey had taken silver at the 1999 World Championships behind Tomas. Macey would go on to score more than 8,600 points at this meet and still come in third.

At another locker I spied Jon-Arnar Magnusson, talented runner and hurdler from Iceland and a two-time World Indoor Championships medalist.

Then there was me, like the rookie who gets drafted late in the season and finds himself in the World Series. I was a junior at a college that most people had not heard of. Somehow I had gotten lucky enough to place third at the USA Championships, and now it was time to compete against these all-time greats.

As I tried to blend in with the wallpaper, I kept thinking, *What am I doing here? I've only been doing the dec for three years. Is this some sort of crazy dream?* I thought I would be exposed as a guy who was in over his head, that all my dreaming and boasting was just a bunch of hot air.

It was the first tme I'd heard anyone speak Czech; as Roman and Tomas spoke to each other, everything they said sounded threatening and tough. They spoke around me as if I were an unfortunately placed pillar. I naturally thought they were talking about me and about how they were going to crush this new, young American. I kept sneaking looks in their bags, seeing vitamin bottles and other items with labels printed in other languages. Everything was new to me.

Then, as if I wasn't rattled enough, Roman suddenly stood up and dropped his pants right next to me, disregarding that we were in a crowded room with female judges and other nonathletes nearby. He stood there buck naked, nonchalantly changing into his competition clothes. *Is anyone else seeing this?* I thought. *Does anyone even care?* Nobody but me seemed to mind.

By the time the competition started, I was frazzled and mentally fatigued from taking it all in. Worse, I didn't realize it then, but the benefits of my warm-up had ebbed away, and my muscles had gotten cold. I had never had to keep warm in a call room, and soon it would show.

We entered the stadium, and as the sun hit my skin and I surveyed the beautiful track in this big arena, I felt a rush of adrenaline. *Okay, I'm going to do this,* I thought, and for a moment my game returned.

But one glance at the guys around me shattered my nerves again. *I'm dead*, I thought.

I lined up for the 100. I was in the fastest heat because of my personal best. I should have won the event outright. Instead, I ran terribly, 10.70, and didn't even win my heat. To this day it's the only 100 that I have lost in a decathlon.

After finishing that event I felt so out of sorts and embarrassed that I made my way off the track and into the room where athletes rest. It had a shower, and I felt so nauseous from anxiety and disappointment that I went in and sat for a while. Within moments I was throwing up repeatedly. The other decathletes poked their heads in and laughed at me.

"Want a dip?" one of them asked, offering me chewing tobacco, which some of the European players chewed. That made me sicker.

Then Kevin showed up. He had tracked me down after seeing me disappear from the field of play.

"How are you doing?" he asked, putting a hand on my shoulder.

"I'm exhausted," I said.

"Let's get you something to eat," he said.

I ate a banana, and between that and having vomited my guts out, I felt much better. Kevin got me back on my feet, and somehow I returned to the track to compete in the next event, the long jump.

Malicious fate had scheduled me to compete right after Tomas. I stood near the back of the runway and observed him as

> I ran terribly. . . .
> It's the only 100
> that I have lost
> in a decathlon.

he warmed up. He seemed so casual, chatting with the other guys. When it was his turn, he blithely turned around to face the runway. He took a few seconds to get the crowd clapping rhythmically in the traditional track and field manner. Then he ran down and launched himself into the air. The crowd in unison said, "Ohhhh!"

He landed in the pit with a jump of 8.07 meters (28 feet 6 inches), which for a decathlete is about as big as it gets. He stood up, stepped out of the pit, saluted the crowd, packed his bag, and walked off the track. It was all over in a matter of seconds. He knew, and we all knew, the jump was big enough that he didn't need to take his other jumps. He could rest for his next event.

It was my first experience with someone being that good. Good enough to say, "Okay, I'm going to jump now," then getting this huge distance and walking off like, "You guys have fun. See you later." It crushed my spirit. And I was next.

I moseyed over, wishing that I were invisible or that the entire crowd would head suddenly to the snack bar. I had no choice but to try to follow Tomas's huge jump. I lined up, looked down the lane, and began running.

It was a clean jump, no foul, but I spent a lot less time in the air than Tomas had. I landed 7.30 meters away. The crowd did nothing, and I felt so embarrassed that my next two jumps were just a blur. The meet had barely started, and I was already an also-ran.

Next was one of my weaker events, the shot put, and I did nothing special there. The high jump should have gone well for me, but I was running on fumes, and I underperformed. Then at the 400, I watched Nool and Macey in an early heat run neck and neck down the home stretch, crossing the line together at 46 seconds, a full second faster than my personal best.

That's what I have to do to be this good? I wondered. I wanted to curl up in a ball and wish myself home. I ran the 400 in 49 seconds, and my wretched day ended.

Kevin and Mom were encouraging, but I couldn't really hear them. It had been one of the worst first days I had ever had, and I had done it in front of the giants of the sport, thousands of fans, and a worldwide television audience. I went to bed wishing I could slip away without anyone knowing I had ever been there.

Bowing Out

The next morning my body felt like it had been hit by a bus. The physical toll was much worse than I had expected. The pain and fatigue made my body feel almost foreign to me, like a gunnysack full of hurt. I sat in the shower for half an hour, as motionless as possible. My neck and back hurt so badly I could hardly get dressed. And I was supposed to go out and do it again.

I sleepwalked through breakfast and reentered the nightmare at the stadium. All the other athletes looked refreshed and raring to go—where their energy came from, I had no idea. My body had not recovered at all.

The day started with the 110-meter hurdles, usually one of my favorite events.

I can't do this, I thought. *I'm so tired that I'm going to hit a hurdle and go down.*

That inspired another thought: *If that happens, at least I won't have to finish.*

As I warmed up, I thought about doing something that had never before crossed my mind: falling intentionally so I could leave the meet. It seemed like an easy way out. I flirted with the idea as we lined up. The gun cracked, and as soon as I began running, I changed my mind and ran full strength, clearing every hurdle. It wasn't my best time, but at least I hadn't taken the shameful alternative of throwing the race.

I threw an unimpressive distance in the discus and then went to the pole vault. I was beyond exhausted, and my right leg was hurting badly enough that I couldn't ignore it. I was concerned it wouldn't function like I needed it to.

The pole vault is an extremely technical event. You take a 15-foot fiberglass pole—thicker in the middle than on the ends—hold it up over your head, and run down the lane. While running, you slowly bring the pole down, plant it in the box, put your hands up over your head, jump off the ground, and follow the pole as it unbends and hurls you upward. You then rock upside down, swing your feet up over your head so you are upside down with the pole in your crotch and your feet facing straight toward the sky. As the pole unbends, you go with it, arch over the bar, and push away from the pole as you fall onto the pit. It is fun but scary and requires a lot of concentration. If you are not there mentally or physically, it won't go well.

I wasn't the best pole vaulter at the time, and I was worried about where I would land if my right leg gave out. I had come down in the box before, after failing to go all the way over, and that hurts. People have died trying to pole vault.

I looked toward the bar and pit, felt the pain in my leg flare again, and started jogging down the runway. I was so tired and distracted by the pain that I didn't even plant the pole in the box. I had failed to visualize myself going through the jump; I no-heighted. I went back a second time and ran through again without planting the pole. The third time I planted the pole but failed to complete the jump.

By then my leg was hurting so badly that I was limping, but more importantly, I had lost the mental game. I had nothing left. Part of me pleaded, *Bryan, this could be your only international competition. There are no guarantees that it gets better than this. This may be the pinnacle of your career.* But I felt so drained, so lifeless, that it didn't matter to me at that moment. A million dollars wouldn't have convinced me to go on. My desire to quit was much stronger than all the rest of my desires combined. I knew I could deal with the failure and disappointment of quitting. It seemed easier than going on.

And my body was providing me with an excuse. My leg was hurting badly. I went with my coaches to a small room under the stadium so that a doctor could check it.

"You've strained it," she said, feeling my quad. "You can try to finish if you want, but I don't think you'll be able to."

Kevin winced, but my heart leaped. *Thank God*, I thought. *Exactly what I want to hear.*

I could hardly have been happier if I'd been released from prison. Kevin said nothing as we made our way to the track to gather my things. I was looking forward to heading to the hotel, taking a hot shower, and getting something to eat. Things were looking suddenly brighter. Then Kevin caught my eye.

"We're not leaving," he said. "You're going to sit in the stands and watch."

I stood there, looking at him in disbelief. He was serious and had that look of "don't push me on this one." I bagged up my things and headed into the stands.

> My desire to quit was much stronger than all the rest of my desires combined. I knew I could deal with the failure and disappointment of quitting. It seemed easier than going on.

Finding a spot high up, I sat as far away from others as I could reasonably get. The meet was in its ninth event, the javelin, and the athletes were warming up for it. The jav seemed to soar as high as my seat on its graceful, powerful trajectory. They were throwing really well, and it was a beautiful thing to watch. I had never watched the javelin in a major competition, and I understood why it is a fan favorite.

I also began to feel an uncomfortable sense of being out of place, as if I was missing what I had come to Edmonton for. Relief vied with regret inside me as I tried to ignore the feelings.

When it was time for the final event, the 1500, I felt almost giddy that I didn't have to run it. The athletes lined up, and at the sound of the gun, they took off like a herd of mustangs. Inevitably some fell behind, and others surged ahead, with knots of runners drafting off each other and strategizing to get the inside lane. At the end each man crossed the finish line and fell onto the ground, spent. I found my heart beating faster as I lived the competition through them.

Tomas Dvorak had won with a monster score of 8,902. Behind him were Nool with 8,815 and the silver, and Macey with 8,603 and the bronze.

I watched the medalists pump their fists and smile as they regained their breath. Then something unexpected happened. Winners and losers alike picked each other up, gave each other high fives, and congratulated each other on finishing. Together they started to jog around the track for a victory lap. They waved at the applauding crowd. It was one of the most awesome displays of brotherhood I had ever seen in sports.

There is pride in just finishing.

For the first time I saw the larger picture of what the decathlon is. It is special and different from every other type of competition. There is pride in just finishing. The medalists probably didn't work any harder than the guys who lost; they just had the better marks that day. The victory lap acknowledged that.

And I had missed being part of it.

You just blew it, I thought. *You should be down there right now. You quit, and you missed something special.* Anger rose in my chest, anger at me. Even if I hadn't done well, I could at least have finished all ten events and run that victory lap. I could have joined the brotherhood instead of sitting in the stands like someone who had bought a ticket that morning. I had given away the privilege of belonging to this elite group.

The lesson Kevin had taught me by forcing me to watch burned inside me.

Looking back, I know I could have gotten through the second day. I have since competed through worse injuries. The strain in my quad was real but also an excuse to quit. That day sitting in the stands in Edmonton I told myself, *I'll never quit a decathlon again unless I absolutely cannot go on.*

It's a promise I have kept.

Learning from Loss

Worlds had been a disaster. But it taught me things I never could have learned at the collegiate or even the national level.

I now understood the importance of focus in the midst of distractions. I understood how important it is to guard your energy. I began to do everything in my power to remove myself from the action and fray of competition so that I would have 100 percent when it came time to compete. This is very difficult to do because the decathlon takes place over twelve or thirteen hours a day, two days in a row. You wake up at 5:00 a.m., start competing at 9:00 a.m., and might run your last event at 10:00 p.m. By the time you take an ice bath, see a doctor, get a massage and maybe an IV if you're dehydrated, then eat dinner, and get a taxi back to your hotel, you are often looking at 2:00 a.m. the next day before you fall asleep. And you might not fall asleep right away.

Then you wake up three hours later, and your last event that day could end at 11:00 p.m. You can't relax or catnap between events; you have to keep up your energy so you are ready for each event. Being in a room with the other athletes during breaks, you face social pressures, noises, conversations, posturing—all of that takes energy. You feel "on" the whole time. Breaks are not restful but are competitions of their own to see who can stay focused and manage their energy properly.

Some meets, such as the USA Championships, have an athlete-friendly schedule, where the events go much quicker and the days finish within six or seven hours. The scores there are almost always higher because you are not dragging out that stress over a twelve-hour period. There is really no way to prepare for the grueling schedule and atmosphere of the World Championships. The only way is to experience it.

Seared into my memory was the knowledge that I would come to a point in every decathlon when I would feel as if I had been dropped over a cliff and would be completely justified in quitting. At that crossroads I would have to decide: Do I quit and come up with an excuse? Or do I keep going through the pain and try to win this thing?

Every single decathlon brings me to that moment. I am tempted to quit. The difference now is that I expect it. Everything in my mind tells me, *Bryan, don't do this. You're taking yourself to hell and back. Just walk away.* But now I know that's normal.

Worlds 2001 was the forge that purified me of early bad habits and taught me lessons I would draw on thereafter. It was in some ways the start of my career. As poorly as I had performed and as doubtful as I was that I would ever compete at that level again, Edmonton was the start of something special.

From that point on I would put together a string of victories that established me at the top of the sport.

EIGHT
THE LESSONS OF A CHAMPION

The lessons that I learned at Edmonton initiated a deep and intense education in the character of a champion. The lessons were not confined to the track. Each one bled over into my spiritual life as well. And the spiritual lessons took on new life when I applied them to my training. Track and faith seemed to constantly feed each other.

Edmonton had helped me understand what competing at the highest level would require. I had to count the cost of finishing a meet. If I was committed to it and loved it, I would not quit when it got hard. By sticking with it, I was honoring and reflecting Christ's love for me. He had committed to me, knowing that I would make bad choices, even run from Him for many years, that I would grieve Him. But He didn't walk away. That was the kind of commitment I needed to have to the sport.

The lesson also worked the other way. If I was committed to track and it was number three on my list of priorities, how much more committed and loving should I be with people like Sarah and my family? How much more committed should I be to Christ? The more I committed to be the best decathlete I could, the higher I set the bar for myself in other areas of life.

My love for God and my love for track fueled each other.

Counting the Costs

One lesson that I continued to learn was how much I have to give up so I can excel in an area. Excellence is a jealous master. It demands an all-encompassing lifestyle. I had already learned that I could not stay up late, live my life however I liked, and then expect to compete well. I have to be in bed by 9:00 p.m. and up at 6:00 a.m. My body and mind need that time to recover. I can't go to late movies, can't stay out with friends, can't even stay up talking with Sarah or reading a book. The sacrifices go further than that. I also have to give up things that other people take for granted: snowboarding, playing pickup games of basketball, riding motorcycles, surfing, bodysurfing, and wrestling with my friends, to name a few.

At APU we had a saying: "Don't break my glass bubble" or "Don't break your glass bubble," which meant, "You're getting a little crazy. Don't hurt your ankle or something." If someone who's not an athlete gets hurt, he or she may have to hobble around in a cast for a while. If I get hurt, it changes my whole career. Every decision I make goes through that test: don't break the glass bubble.

Arguing can be exhausting, so I became more ready to apologize to Sarah and settle conflicts early. You might say that committing to track made me a better boyfriend. I couldn't afford to get to the track tired because I had stayed up trying to win a point in some disagreement that ultimately didn't matter. I had to stay focused.

Giving up fun stuff to protect my track career has been hard at times, but it has also taught me a valuable spiritual lesson that the apostle Paul wrote about in one of his letters:

> Don't you realize that in a race everyone runs, but only one person gets the prize? So run to win! All athletes are disciplined in their training. They do it to win a prize that will fade away, but we do it for an eternal prize. So I run with purpose in every step. I am not just shadowboxing. I discipline my body like an athlete, training it to do what it should. (1 Corinthians 9:24–27)

I was living that scripture in very practical terms. I also applied it to my mind and spirit. If I wanted to succeed spiritually, I would have to guard my heart and mind, be vigilant about what I allowed myself to view or listen to or think about. I had to strip away extraneous thoughts and focus on one thing: Christ. That became a lifestyle for me on and off the track.

My days of carelessness were gone. Now was the time to be intentional, about track and about my walk with Christ. Anything less was not worthy of Him.

Establishing Routines

I also underwent a transformation from a guy who hated routines to a guy who relied on them. When I was in high school, my parents had tried to get me on a regular schedule, but I wanted to be footloose and spontaneous. I did what I liked with no plan before a meet. I did nothing to protect my mind or conserve my energy. But as I advanced in track and began to compete with professionals, I observed that the difference between successful athletes and those who fell short of their potential was structure. I started putting a routine together through trial and error.

I had noticed that many athletes wore headphones before a competition. I thought that looked cool, so in high school I started wearing headphones and listening to loud, aggressive music. That pumped me up, and I thought, *I'm going to destroy everybody at this meet.* I fostered a crazy, dominating attitude toward competition. It took a while to realize that this music and attitude were more of a distraction than anything because they wasted energy. So I started to experiment with different music, and to my surprise I found the music styles that helped me concentrate and relax most were worship music and country. Worship music puts my spirit at ease, focuses me, and reminds me of what's important in life and that I am not in control. Country music is just lighthearted and fun and makes me feel as if I'm at home. It reminds me of my family, hunting and fishing, and things I enjoy.

Then I started experimenting with putting together small routines before and during competition. If I didn't compete as well, I dropped certain elements. Helpful routines, I kept. Eventually I had created finely honed routines in every part of my life.

The morning of competition I put my headphones on, go for a light jog to wake up my body, and take a shower. I don't talk to anyone, not even my coaches. Then I have oatmeal, and we all head to the track. I do it all in the same order and the same way. It's not superstition; it is a way of relaxing by doing predictable things. When I get into competition, I go into one long routine made up of a series of small routines. I start by walking the track and visualizing myself doing well in every event. When it's time to compete, I have a routine for each event.

Take the long jump, for example. I stand at the back of the runway and do a particular stretch. Then I visualize jumping and count my cadence—one and two and three and four and five and six and seven and eight and nine and ten. I visualize myself jumping on ten.

Then I step to my mark. I count my cadence one more time, rock back, and run.

Having a routine in every event flips the switch and tells my body and mind, "Okay, here we go. He's doing all the things we do before this event. Time to make it happen." These routines keep me focused and at ease. I don't have to stress about what to do; I just do it.

Some people have the idea that athletes try to outperform their marks in competition. That's not the case, at least it's not for me. The goal is simply to do what I do every day in practice. In other words, I bring my practice routine to the meet. That means that if I execute the same as I do when there's no pressure, I'll hit my marks when it counts. I go in thinking, *All I'm going to do today is what I do every single day in practice.* My rule is to try hard and push myself in practice, but in competition just do what I normally do. Don't push too hard. Don't overexert to try to get some personal best. Just execute.

My routines became a shield against the excitement and the ups and downs that inevitably happen in the course of two days of competition. My routines don't allow me to become distracted by the energy of the fans, the sound of the cheering, or the size of the stadium.

> Routines keep me focused and at ease. I don't have to stress about what to do; I just do it.

When everything is flowing well, I don't even think about the routines. I just go through them. But when something unexpected happens and the competition gets hard or stressful, that's when I fall back on them. If I'm doing discus and have a bad throw, I stop, clear my mind, and say, "What do I do now? What is my routine?" I think it through, remind myself of the steps, then get into the ring, swing my arm three times, take a deep breath, wind up, and throw. Almost always that throw will be okay. The routine is my pattern for consistent success.

My routine probably would be different if I were a different kind of athlete. For example, if I were running one event, say the 100, I might want to listen to loud music to build myself up for a single explosion of energy. I might want the energy of the fans to pump me up. But because I am doing the decathlon and managing energy for twelve-hour days with three hours of sleep, I simply cannot give energy away. A precise routine conserves my energy.

I have become such a creature of routine that without one I get lost in my day and am easily upset. I feel out of balance. I developed routines even for my rest times. Without them I found myself sitting around the house wondering what I should do. In college I noticed that when I didn't have practice, I didn't get homework done. I had more time but was getting less done. When I had practice, my routine took me through the day, and I did better in all areas of life.

I even have macro-routines that go throughout the year. In the fall training slows down a little bit, then picks up in the new year, and accelerates in the spring. Then I taper a bit, and training changes somewhat so I can be at my peak for the important summer meets. There is an annual cycle, and as I later prepared for the 2004 and 2008 Olympics, I even developed a quadrennial cycle. The micro-routines and macro-routines all work together.

Sometimes I can't believe I have become such a structured guy, given my island heritage and my tendency to want to relax without a lot of demands. Then I remember my grandfather, Jiji, and it makes more sense. He couldn't have built his business without a good deal of structure. Indeed, I found myself in his routine for many years—early mornings and long days. Maybe my reliance on routines isn't so surprising after all.

Routines also shaped my life off the track. Without thinking too much about it, I had established spiritual routines that built strength into my life: Bible reading, devotions, D-group, church attendance, regular prayer, and worship. I also discovered relational routines with Sarah that helped us meet each other's needs and reduce the volatility that can accompany any new relationship.

I began to notice in the Bible that Jesus had routines during His earthly life. People call them the spiritual disciplines. It made perfect sense to me. Jesus' task was more demanding than any decathlon. His ministry required everything He had physically and mentally. I saw in His routines the strategic approach I was taking to life and to track. He was conserving His energy, structuring His time, making sure everything got done, and always returning to the basics.

Proper routines, in athletics and in life, are foundational to success.

One Step at a Time

The painful experience in Edmonton also taught me that life works best when you take it one step at a time. Some mornings it's a big step for me just to get out of bed. It's another big step to get into the shower. It's another big step to get dressed. After a series of steps, soon I am in the weight room and actually accomplishing something with my day.

Every day I focus on little goals, not big ones. I don't think about my four-year plan, three-year plan, two-year plan, one-year plan, monthly plan, or weekly plan. I think of my daily plan. Big goals can seem impossible and get in the way of accomplishing little goals. Trying to run the 100 in 10.10 seconds sounds far-fetched. But trying to run it in 10.40 doesn't. So my daily goal is to run it in 10.40. When I accomplish that consistently, my daily goal becomes 10.35 and so on. Over time those little goals add up.

Some athletes try to rush excellence. They take steroids because it speeds up the process of recovery, allowing them to work out harder, longer, and more frequently than they otherwise would. A guy on steroids can get in two days of practice on one day. But in the end he wrecks his body. That is a terrible price to pay because the improvement wasn't real.

He tried to take more than one step at a time.

I began to apply the same strategy to my walk with Christ. To be Christlike can seem impossible to me—unless I take it one step at a time. Maybe today I sense God is helping me resist saying a harsh word to someone in my fatigue or resist some other temptation. My goal is to work in that direction. I rarely have more than one goal a day in my spiritual life. I keep it very simple. If I can accomplish that, then I move on to the next goal. Every victory gets me closer to the character of Christ.

Breaking Things Down

One of my knacks as an athlete is the ability to break things down to their most basic elements. Maybe it is an island mentality or just my personality, but I keep things as simple as possible. Some people overcomplicate things. They get lost in all the moving parts. I try to do the opposite. I have discovered that most things in life and in track can be pulled apart, understood, and worked on as individual steps.

Every event I do is a series of basic movements. The best coaches in the sport understand this. It does not help to tell me to run faster or throw harder. I need to know what the components of that are. One time a coach told me to rock back faster in the pole vault. After half a day of hearing this and not understanding what he meant, I finally got exasperated. "I know what you're telling me to do, but how do I do it?" I asked. "I know what the end result is supposed to look like. I know what A looks like and B looks like. I need to know what happens in the space between them. Give me one thing to concentrate on."

When he broke it down into individual steps, suddenly I saw what I needed to do. I could execute it.

Learning each event is like learning to walk. Babies don't walk first; they don't even crawl. They start by rolling over, then pushing up, then sitting up, and so on until they are scampering around the room. Most of life is that way for me. No matter how much knowledge or information I have, it doesn't do me any good unless I can break it down into achievable steps. Then I practice those steps again and again until they become natural.

Another example is ankle positioning and posture when I run. I used to point my toes down as opposed to keeping my ankles nice and locked. My poor form made me prone to injuries and kept me from running as efficiently and as fast as I could. The only way to keep my feet from dangling was to drill and drill to fix that one problem. I had to think about it and work on it repeatedly.

In my walk with Christ, I do the same thing. I seize on one question or one habit and think about it for weeks or months until I solve it. I break it down into its various components, just as I did when I was trying to figure out what love is and just as I do on the track. I debate each possibility. Then once I figure it out, I practice and practice until it becomes second nature to me.

Doing Things the Right Way May Feel Wrong at First

As I practiced correct techniques and habits on the track and in my spiritual life, I quickly learned that the right way of doing things almost always felt unnatural the first time. Why? Because I had been doing it wrong for so long. Change feels awkward. You get so used to the wrong way that you resist the right way.

For example, before I got to college, I used to walk very open, dragging the backs of my slippers on the ground. My high school coach told me I needed to correct that and point my feet forward. So every day I retrained myself by walking on the lane line with my feet facing forward. It felt completely wrong. My body felt out of alignment, I felt pressure on certain parts of my legs, and I woke up sore because I was not used to using those muscles. But I needed to do it. Over time my mind accepted it as natural.

Another example involved the shot put. Early on when I was a college athlete, Coach Barnett kept telling me, "Keep your arms back and your hips closed." He told me that when I was gliding through the middle of the ring, I was turning my hips prematurely. That's called being open, and it robs you of the coil or slingshot effect.

Finally after he'd yelled "Keep your hips closed" enough times, I fought back and said, "I am! I can feel it." "No, you're not," he said, and to prove it, he videotaped me. Only then did I see what he saw: my hips were wide open. It was eerie to see it happening on the tape because my "feeling" told me that I was doing it right and that my hips were closed. I had to learn a new feeling and reprogram my mind to accept it as natural.

> Change feels awkward. You get so used to the wrong way that you resist the right way.

I can't think of a single event that I naturally did correctly from the start. Almost every one got turned upside down in training. That's humbling for a young athlete who already has had some success. But to do it right and excel, I had to learn it correctly.

The parallel to my spiritual life was obvious. As my training worked bad habits out of me, it became easier for me to accept that I was wrong and needed training in other areas of life. Partying had felt natural to me for years, but it was wrong. I had to retrain my mind. Abusing substances had felt natural to me, but it wasn't. Sleeping in on Sundays and on my D-group days had felt natural, but I needed to instill a new habit of getting up early to honor the Lord.

Some people wait for the Christian life to seem natural to them. I know from experience that it never will at first. Having faith is believing something is right before it feels right. That's a recipe for success in every area of life.

Finding Mentors and Trusting Them

I had to trust not only the techniques I was learning; I had to trust my coaches. I have four primary coaches: Kevin Reid, Mike Barnett, Rana Reider, and Paul Doyle, who is also my manager. Coach Barnett coaches my throws, Rana, my jumps, and Paul writes my workout plan. Kevin oversees it all. (For some reason I have always called Mike "Coach Barnett" and Kevin, Rana, and Paul by their first names. I'm not sure why, and it doesn't imply any difference in respect.)

Each of these guys is a role model to me in addition to being a coach. Our relationships are based on trust. I have gone to each one of them for personal and spiritual advice. Kevin, in particular, has been a friend as well as a coach. I have babysat his kids. He knows me very well, probably better than anybody else in athletic terms. And that's critical to his success as my primary coach.

Kevin has to know me well enough that he can tell when I come to the track distracted mentally. He can read my attitude quickly and ask, "Everything all right? You seem a little down today." If I am feeling tired or upset, he might make adjustments to practice so I don't overdo it or carelessly injure myself. It is possible when you are stressed out and tired to push yourself too hard and get hurt unless someone steps in and says, "Whoa, whoa. I can tell you are tired and not here today. Let's lay off." At other times Kevin knows me well enough to tell me to snap out of my funk and get to work. He has the most important job of all my coaches because he manages my daily routine. Without him I am lost in my training.

Though I trust all of my coaches, I have a healthy back-and-forth relationship with them. We push and challenge each other. We'll argue and even yell a little bit, and they will get stern with me if I need it. I tell them exactly how I feel, and they do the same. We are not reserved by any means. But that's good because I need to understand what I am doing, and they need to understand what I am having trouble understanding. We work it out and come back together. We have that common understanding guys have when you can yell at each other then put it aside. It doesn't harm our relationship; it strengthens it.

One thing I argue about with Kevin all the time is whether I am doing too much or not enough. This is a big issue in training. You are constantly walking the line of overtraining or undertraining. There are days when I don't feel that I have done enough. Kevin will say, "Let's be done. You had a great workout. Let's not overdo it."

I'll counter, "But I didn't do the whole workout."

"Let's stop anyway," he'll say.

"No," I'll say, "I'm going to finish the workout."

Other times he will want me to do more when my body hurts and I want to quit.

One time I recall clearly going against Kevin's advice. My body felt wrecked from a workout, but I wanted to finish it anyway. He told me to stop early before I got hurt. "You need to listen to me and trust me," he said. "I tell you this because I don't want you to take your body to a place where it won't recover."

I defied him and finished the workout anyway. Sure enough, the next week I was so destroyed that I couldn't even train. I had pushed my muscles and joints so far that my body shut down for mandatory repairs. If I had taken a recovery period as Kevin recommended, I wouldn't have fouled up my training regimen and set myself back. I should have listened.

I have the same kind of relationship with God. I am not one of those people who takes everything without questioning. I am heartened that in the Bible, many of the great men and women argued with God. Abraham, Jacob, David, and many others had ongoing discussions with Him. Abraham tried to persuade God to spare Sodom and Gomorrah. Jacob literally wrestled with God all night. Jesus pleaded with the Father in the Garden of Gethsemane the night before His death. Many, many times throughout Scripture, God invites discussion and is even open to persuasion.

Why does He do it? I don't know. Obviously He knows best. I do know that this kind of relationship is satisfying and strengthening to me. I get no satisfaction out of blindly following God or my coaches without applying my mind to what they say. In fact, I think that kind of passivity can be dangerous and lead people to follow false prophets and cults. I have seen this happen to athletes who start listening to a new coach and get wooed away from the training regimen and coach who made them successful in the first place. They head in a new, "exciting" direction and ruin their training and sometimes their career.

People do the same with their faith. They think it is an exercise of faith to accept whatever a certain spiritual leader says without examining it. I don't see it that way. If I am reading the Bible and asking questions about the sermons I hear and the books I read and the advice I get, I feel less likely to be duped. I want to be actively engaged and not just accept what people say without inspection. I am constantly looking for mentors, guys I can ask about everything from the deep questions to practical stuff. I have a hunger for wisdom and advice.

On the track I trust my coaches because I don't know everything about training and I believe God has put them in my life. I know I can't succeed alone. But this is my career we're talking about, and I am still responsible for going out and researching my sport by attending camps and talking to other coaches and athletes about their approaches. We also add other coaches into my regimen, from time to time, for events such as the pole vault, and they help bring in a fresh perspective. It is always nice to hear how they do things differently to try to achieve the same result. And there are times when one of our temporary coaches says something in such a way that I suddenly understand it after banging my head against the wall for months.

> **God invites discussion and is even open to persuasion.**

These habits and many more helped me to transform myself as an athlete and a follower of Christ. My life became an act of devotion and worship. The gift and responsibility I had been given as an athlete weren't for me anymore; they were for God. In a hard workout I would catch myself saying, "Okay, Lord, I can't do it. I need Your help." Or I would talk to Him about doing well in the next run or throw or jump.

I had more joy in practice and performance than ever before. In working out and striving for excellence, I was giving my gift back to God and saying, "Use my body so I can bring glory and honor to You." Being a champion in life led me to become a champion on the track, not the other way around. My track career and faith became intertwined. God constantly used my career as a tool to teach me about my walk with Him.

That's when I started to believe I really could make another world championship team and even go to the Olympics. I didn't believe I could win a gold medal because my mind told me that dreams still didn't come true. But I thought I could perform at a higher level than ever before.

With all those habits in place, I was ready to step onto the world stage again. And unlike what I had done at Edmonton, this time I wasn't going to quit.

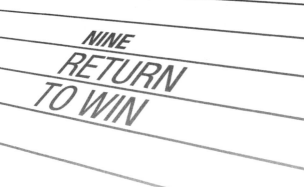

NINE
RETURN TO WIN

Every time your score goes up, you wonder whether you have peaked. You don't know what you are capable of until you do it. I *thought* I could run faster and jump farther, but could I really? How big was my upside? Even if I could score better in the individual events, could I consistently put them all together in the decathlon? Or had my score at the 2001 USA Championships been a fluke?

The verdict was still out. Some people discouraged me from believing I could do better. "The chances of your winning a gold medal or becoming a professional athlete are pretty thin," one well-meaning acquaintance told me. "If I were you, I would get out of this track thing and devote yourself to your schoolwork." I didn't accept that advice and not just because I had never had a great love for school. I knew there was more for me in the sport.

In 2002, in spite of injuries to my elbow and shoulder, I went back to competing at the college level and led APU to national indoor and outdoor championships, the first time a "team double" had ever been accomplished. I was recognized as an NAIA Outstanding Performer after winning the pentathlon and the long jump at the outdoor meet. By this time I was a twenty-three-time NAIA All-American. Three years in a row my score at the end of the year was the highest collegiate score, even in the NCAA. But true to form, few paid attention to that. They never took the NAIA seriously. So in spite of my marks, I continued to fly under the radar.

Victory—and Decision Time

I qualified for the USA Championships again, and this time, to my great satisfaction and surprise, I won silver, besting Kip Janvrin and Phil McMullen and coming in behind Tom Pappas, who at that time was dominating the field. I scored 8,200 points, which I privately took as the first indication that I could consistently score above 8,000. I had done it twice. There was no reason I couldn't do it again.

The meet was also memorable for me because Dan O'Brien, then thirty-five years old and six years past his Olympic medal, competed in many of the events. I had never had the opportunity to compete against him, and it was a privilege to be on the same field. I spent free moments watching him warm up and compete. He was in third place after four events but pulled out of the 400 due to a foot injury he had been nursing.

Strangely, because the dec was held at a separate site away from the other track and field events, the stands were virtually empty. The only people present were the athletes, coaches, and officials. When we ran or jumped, the only sounds we heard were the wind, our own grunts and movements, and our coaches clapping or shouting from somewhere in the bleachers. I didn't care. I was having the time of my life. If success is a measure of enjoyment, it's no wonder I did so well.

The season was now over since World Championships happen only in odd years, and I focused on my relationship with Sarah and applying the lessons I had learned on the track to my life. The off-season was quiet.

Coming into 2003, I expected to do better than ever. I'd had a good winter of training and performed well in early competitions. At the USA Outdoor Championships, held at Stanford University, I pushed my score up to 8,482 and took the silver again behind Tom Pappas, who was becoming a familiar presence at the top of the medal stand. The meet had started strong for me with a 10.43 in the 100. But Tom was having a great meet as well. He ran a good time in the 100, which is usually not his strongest event.

I went out and had a good long jump, but he had an even better one, a remarkable 7.96 meters (26 feet 1.5 inches). He is an out-standing shot-putter, so he excelled there, and his high jump was an incredible 221 centimeters (7 feet 3 inches). The next day he pole vaulted 5.10 meters (16 feet 9 inches) and thus completed one of the best jump series ever recorded in a decathlon. It was a meet worthy of a champion.

Both of us prepared to go to the World Championships in Paris, but first I had important decisions to make. In May I had graduated from college but stayed on the APU training sched-ule, working out with the team. APU let me use the weight rooms and track and gave me a master key to the facilities. Yet again I was receiving a benefit I never would have received at a Division I school. The overlooked NAIA continued to bless me in ways I could not have predicted coming out of high school. APU was a major part of my *ohana*.

I could no longer live on the campus, however, and I didn't have any scholarship funds. Even though I had won bronze and silver at the past two USA Championships, I didn't have an endorsement contract. And if I wanted to keep competing, I would have to find a way to support myself. As a bachelor, I didn't need much—but I needed something.

A friend suggested that I seek sponsors from among people I knew and basically ask them to invest in my career by giving me monthly support. The idea scared me to death, but the alternative—working a job or giving up my career—seemed worse.

I put together a business plan on my computer, added some photos, and answered every question I thought investors would have: "What is this going to cost me? Why should I give any money to you? What are your costs? What benefit will I get out of this?" I listed all my expenses, what I paid for rent and groceries and more. It was an austere budget. I listed the meets where I had competed, the meets I intended to enter, my daily training schedule, and more. It read like a business assessment of my life. The message, I hoped, was clear: I'll be a good steward of your money.

Some friends who were in business invited me to make presentations to their money guys, and I found myself sitting in conference rooms at various companies. I was more nervous than I had ever been at a sporting event. I took them through the business plan I had prepared, and they nodded noncommittally. I had no idea what they were thinking.

It's possible they had spoken to each other beforehand and agreed to give me money regardless. In any case I went through the whole presentation, and each person or corporation I asked committed to give me a certain amount per month. I had promised to treat them like sponsors and print up a T-shirt advertising their businesses, but they really were not interested in that. They just saw a local kid with a dream and wanted to help make that come true. Their support was pivotal. Instead of dividing my energies, I was able to train full-time.

New Focus

Being able to give my full attention to training turned out to be incredibly important because I had a lot of work to do. My APU coaches stuck with me after I graduated. Because I had medaled three years in a row at the USA Outdoor Championships, they knew, and I knew, that I had the potential to go even further in the sport than any of us had fully envisioned. We began to think of how to reach higher goals. We looked much more closely at what to improve and became targeted and specific about my technique in each event.

I worked with Coach Barnett on my throws. He knows the science of the sport inside and out and always has his nose in an athletic journal. He is up on every technique. Coach Barnett is an incredible guy. He has also been a spiritual mentor to me, someone who thinks deeply, not just about performance and competition but about living for God. His approach to life and the sport is perfect for me.

As we started to focus on areas that needed work, Coach Barnett recognized that I have one primary disadvantage compared to other decathletes: my size. I am only 5 feet 10 and weigh just 175 pounds. But within that small package, I have something that most other athletes do not:

> We looked much more closely at what to improve and became targeted and specific about my technique in each event.

explosive speed and power. So instead of using the mechanical advantage of long arms and legs—which coaches call *levers*—I use speed and power. I have nothing else.

Up to that point my power and natural ability had masked flaws in my technique. Coach Barnett, being the great coach he is, saw my technique clearly. He wasn't fooled by a decent result. He watched my feet, body, hands, head, and every movement I made to get a result. In each of my throws—shot put, discus, and javelin—he saw room for improvement.

I was still something of a novice in my throws since I had not done them in high school—the shot put, discus, and javelin all were still relatively new to me. The good news was that I had not learned any bad habits. The bad news was that I had not learned any good habits, either. My mistakes were due to lack of knowledge, not poor training.

Coach Barnett started with the shot put. The goal was not to make me the best shot-putter in the world—I would never compete with specialists in that sport—but to make me one of the best decathlon shot-putters in the world, which is a whole different matter. To throw the shot, athletes use their core power and legs to push and release the shot at just the right moment, putting all the energy of the throw onto the sixteen-pound metal ball.

The main mistake I was making was in my timing. I was releasing my energy too early, exploding in the middle of the ring. By the time I hit the edge and launched the shot, my power was no longer at full strength. It had peaked a fraction of a second too soon.

In any event, particularly the throws, it is easy to mess up in the first millisecond. Coach Barnett could see that, but at first I couldn't. If I threw poorly, I thought it was something I did at the very end, but Coach Barnett pointed out that I had made a misstep at the very beginning, which carried through and affected every movement that followed. He took me back to the beginning, slowed the process down, and helped me see what I was doing wrong.

"You have to light the fuse and let it burn slowly," he said. "You don't want it to explode until you get through the ring and plant your left toe near the toe board for the throw. It's about patience and not using all the energy getting there. Like a grenade, you pull the pin, but it doesn't explode immediately. It has to go off at the right time. Don't start with an explosion. Tell yourself, 'Hold, hold, hold, *now.*'"

Coach Barnett made me pick a spot eight feet behind the ring and keep my eyes on that spot as long as possible while I drove to the toe board, gliding forward with a half-rotation of the right leg, and released. It took a lot of monotonous footwork and drill after drill to help me understand what a correct technique felt like and to get it into my muscle memory. There was much more to throwing than I had realized.

"It's not just about speed and power," Coach Barnett told me. "It's about every part of your body being in position and moving correctly. You have to step correctly, rotate correctly, and have your head and shoulders in the correct position. At one point the left side of your body has to stop rotating while your right side continues. That requires flexibility and minute coordination. Move too fast, get a leg out of position to your body, arch too soon, rotate improperly, or hold your chin too low, and the power will be applied in the wrong direction, and the throw won't go as far."

> "Light the fuse and let it burn slowly . . . Tell yourself, 'Hold, hold, hold, *now.*'"

When I first understood all this, I said, "There are so many tiny things to think about. How can I possibly do them all?"

But Coach Barnett was firm: "It's not only possible, but you have to do it if you want to improve your marks. Throws are about torque, about putting as much speed and power as possible on the implement at the right time. And that requires right technique. It is never a matter of luck or chance."

I had to become teachable as never before. I had to learn to go along with changes that felt awkward and wrong, right in the middle of practice. Sometimes I wouldn't feel the proper technique right away, and I'd get frustrated. Coach Barnett would take me through the movements frame by frame. With each frame he would stop me.

"Okay, what do you feel right now? Hold the feeling in your mind and muscles. Ready? Next frame. Now, what do you feel?"

He would position me again and again like a mannequin. We moved backward and forward, frame by frame until I got the sequence into my mind and muscles.

After a while, when I missed a throw, Coach Barnett didn't have to tell me what I did wrong. I told him.

Intensive Training

I spent more time in the weight room, doing bench presses and military presses, which is lifting a weighted bar over the head while in a standing position. Coach Barnett wrote my weight program and worked closely with me. I worked with a medicine ball and did all sorts of strength exercises to improve my rotation.

Coach Barnett was careful not to let me build too much muscle, which would drag me down in the running and jumping events. There is a balance for a decathlon athlete. If he is too light, he has no power to throw the implements. If he is too heavy, he is a plodding runner and jumper. For me, 178 pounds was a good balance. I was still able to bench press 350 pounds and squat 550 pounds, more than I had thought possible for someone my size.

We worked next on the discus. Like the shot put, the discus has several specific steps and requires a great sense of spatial awareness. Unlike the glide motion of the shot put, the discus is a 360-degree rotation. There are more movements and, therefore, more that can go wrong. My problem at the time was rotating too quickly and falling into the middle of the ring, leaving little power for the actual throw. I spent a lot of frustrating days launching the discus into the netting instead of the sector (that is, the playing field) because I was out of position and releasing energy too soon.

Once again I had to learn to enter the ring slowly and correctly, not to rush into the driving phase, and bring all the torque onto the discus at the moment of release. We did more stepping drills than I thought possible, feeling where my body was with each step, putting my foot in exactly the right spot, keeping my head and torso and limbs in the right position with each movement, and then finally putting it all together for a throw.

Most decathletes struggle with the discus more than with the other throws, and now I understood why. But soon I was throwing 180 feet, which for a decathlete of my size is pretty good. In the coming years the training would prove itself in impressive fashion.

Then came the javelin. I already had a decent arm, but my technique needed a lot of work. When you watch someone throw the javelin, it can seem as easy as throwing a baseball. But there is much more to it, and it is very difficult to hit the right positions.

When you start, you are holding the 1.7-pound spear behind you, so it feels as if you are running away from it, as if the javelin is chasing you. So I had to work on getting my armpit to the sky—as Coach Barnett reminded me again and again—meaning I had to arch my back and turn my arm up so my armpit was almost facing up.

When you make it to the end of the runway and get into the penultimate step, your body should be parallel to the runway; you rotate your right foot and plant your left, which catapults you into the air, and all of that energy is released through your shoulder. You can't pull down on the jav at the end of the throw, as you do with a baseball. You have to throw and release it on the way up, at 45 or 46 degrees. When the jav leaves your hand, it should almost disappear, as if the handle is traveling through the center of that tip. Coach Barnett calls it "throwing it through the point."

If that makes it sound simple, it's not. If my legs, lower body, upper body, shoulders, arms, wrists, fingers, or head is out of position, it affects the speed and position of the jav as it flies. Again, success is determined by a multitude of tiny movements, each of which I had to train myself to feel. Coach Barnett again broke the throw into steps, and we worked them endlessly until the sequence began to feel natural to me.

Coach Barnett calls the technique a *train wreck* because the final motion is like trains colliding. The body stops and all the torque is transferred through the feet, legs, hips, core, shoulder, arm, and hand into this spear, which hurtles out like a lightning bolt. The javelin is the most dangerous of the throws because you can injure yourself easily. (You can also injure others. In 2007, a javelin thrown by a female athlete hit Roman Sebrle; thankfully it caused only a minor wound.) You can injure your back, shoulder, or elbow and end your season in one throw if you are not in correct position. The massive energy can travel through the wrong muscle fibers and tear them apart.

For that reason we didn't do nearly as much javelin practice as we did shot put or discus. We might practice the other throws two or three times a week, but we did the jav every couple of weeks and only at 75 percent strength, practicing in the grass for softness. To this day I rarely go 100 percent on the jav, except in meets. And every time I do I know I am risking a potentially career-ending injury.

With all this focused practice I became much more technically clean in all my events, and my coaches and I could see that I was better than I had ever been. But we had yet to hit my ceiling.

Returning to Worlds

In 2003, I did some meets around California and continued to train with the college team. I was ready to compete on my second world championship team, and this time, after getting silver behind Tom Pappas, I vowed it would be different. I wouldn't be spooked by everything new or by the other athletes. I would go in and compete my way, using the lessons I had learned at Edmonton. I wanted to prove that I belonged on the world stage. Scoring 8,400 at the USA Outdoor Championships had bolstered my confidence. In Paris I would make a name for myself.

Paris was one of the most attractive cities I had ever seen. I instantly fell in love with it. When not training, my coaches and I walked through the Louvre, went to the Eiffel Tower, and ate at countless restaurants and corner cafés that lined the streets. But the world was still tense because of 9/11, so we were warned to be careful not to advertise that we were Americans while walking around town. We didn't wear our USA gear, and we traveled everywhere in groups. We were in virtual lockdown at our hotel, behind fencing and with guards stationed around the bottom level. They wouldn't let anyone in unless they produced a U.S. credential. I had never seen such tight security.

I was in the best shape of my life and my practices showed it. My coaches told me I looked great, I told them I felt great, and all of us were confident I could give Tom Pappas and the international athletes a run for the gold.

Then, four days before the meet, in my last practice, on the last hurdle of my last repetition I stepped wrong, twisted sideways a bit, and hit the hurdle hard. I felt a pinch in my leg and stopped, lying down on the track and thinking, *I can't believe I just did that. I hope it's nothing serious.* But it hurt. Holding my leg, I rolled on the ground.

My coaches came over.

"What happened?" Kevin and Rana asked.

"I just felt my hamstring go."

"You're kidding. How serious?"

"I don't know."

I got up and tried to walk off without limping too badly so the other athletes and coaches wouldn't know I was injured. We went straight to the U.S. doctors. By that time I was panicking a little bit. A sober silence had come over my coaches. One doctor put me on a table and felt my leg.

> In Paris I would make a name for myself.

"There's a knot in the hamstring," he said, grimacing. "There's no way you'll be able to compete."

I looked at Kevin and Rana, and all I could think was, *You've got to be kidding. I'm in the best shape of my life. How could I possibly not be able to compete?*

"What about treatment?" Kevin and Rana asked the doctor.

"We can ice it and do some therapy to help with blood flow and pain," the doctor replied. "But I don't think it'll be enough."

His words devastated me. But Rana wasn't ready to give up. After we left the room, he said in disgust, "Forget this. We're not listening to these doctors. We're going to someone else."

He was upset that the doctors would throw in the towel so quickly. So we met with the Canadian doctor, who seemed more hopeful.

"Yeah, I can feel the divot, but let's try to get you back," he said.

I embarked on a regimen of active release therapy (ART), acupuncture, and massage twice a day for four days. I was skeptical about it working, but it was the only option. An athlete doesn't come back that fast from pulling a hamstring, and we all knew the odds were long. I didn't work out, not even to jog.

Our plan was to wait until the morning of the competition to see if I could do anything. That day I awakened to a beautiful Paris morning and did my normal routine. I got another round of treatment. When I jogged, my leg was okay. I did some strides—still okay. I held back because I didn't want to blow it out in practice.

"I think I can run," I told Kevin. "I just don't know how hard."

We headed to the stadium with Worlds 2001 still fresh in my mind. I wasn't going to let that happen again; I was going to do everything I could to compete. No quitting this time. I walked and then jogged slowly to see what my leg could handle. It felt all right. I skipped a little and did some drills but held back so I wouldn't stress the leg too quickly.

> I'm in the best shape of my life. How could I possibly not be able to compete?

Then I tried a stride at 50 percent. It felt fine. I did another stride at 60 percent. Still fine. I worked up to 85 percent or so, and the leg handled it. I still had a hitch in my step because I couldn't let go of the thought that I had injured it. But my confidence began to grow, and I thought I might actually be able to compete.

"Let's call it there and see if we can do something in this meet," said Kevin. We agreed that I would go 85 percent in each event and see how far I went.

I lined up for the first event, the 100, and thought, *Here goes nothing*. The gun went off, and I found myself running hard but still wondering about my leg. At 30 meters I didn't feel pain, so I ran harder. At 50 meters it was still doing all right, so I ran harder. By the end of the race, I was running almost full speed, but I still had a limp. I clocked a time of 10.51, the fastest time of anyone. I won the event.

"I can't believe I just ran that time," I told my coaches quietly as we huddled near the bleachers. They were as cautiously excited as I was.

"Can you feel the leg?" they asked.

"Not at all," I said. "I was thinking about it the whole time, though. I'd have run 10.30 if I'd had all my wheels."

"Let's do this," Kevin said. "We're going to have a great meet."

I disappeared briefly into a private room to get acupuncture. At the next event, the long jump, I took it easy in warm-ups and jumped a personal best, 7.75 meters (25 feet 5.5 inches). But my leg suddenly blared with pain two steps out from the launch. I landed okay, saw the white flag and the impressive distance I had managed, and went back under the bleachers to my coaches.

"I just felt my leg go," I said, starting to panic.

Kevin grimaced, and Rana ran to get the doctor. I met them under the stadium and got more acupuncture and massage, and the doctor taped my leg up so I couldn't open it all the way even if I wanted to.

In the shot put, though my leg was wrapped up and painful, I came out and threw 15 meters (49 feet 2.5 inches), more than 3 feet farther than my personal best. All I could figure was that I was in such good shape that my body was compensating for the injury. With an injured leg I was leading the competition after three events.

"Bryan, you're in this thing," Kevin whispered. "Let's keep it going. You've got a shot if you keep having a meet like you're having now."

There was a long scheduled break between the morning and evening sessions, as with every World Championship and Olympic competition. The idea was to take a siesta, go under the bleachers, eat, drink, and rest.

But my leg was getting worse, and as I rested, it got tighter and tighter. After a while I tried to warm it up, but it resisted. During the warm-up for the high jump, it hurt much worse, and I couldn't open up my stride. The pain was hard to ignore. I went into the event and made do with a middling score but lost the lead. My leg was not kidding around anymore.

"I don't see how I'm going to run this 400," I told my coaches.

"Just do your best," they said, their optimism diminished.

I lined up, ready to do whatever I needed to get through the race. I was not going to back off now. I would protect the leg a little at first and open it up later on, just as I had done in the 100. The gun went off, and I leaped off the line a little slower than usual. In the initial burst I thought I might make it all the way to the finish line, but four or five steps in, my leg shrieked with pain, and I knew I might injure it much worse by continuing. I couldn't even get up to 85 percent. I pulled up 30 meters down the track and walked back to the start lane near the tunnel. I found my coaches at the bleachers.

> With an injured leg I was leading the competition after three events.

"It's okay, Bryan. It's part of the game," Kevin said. "Remember this feeling. We'll come back stronger next year. Next year is the one that matters."

He was referring to the 2004 Olympics. I could hardly respond because of the emotions caught in my throat.

"If you're going to get hurt, this is the year," Rana said, his hand on my shoulder. "It may not make sense now, but there's a reason God takes you through a situation like this. He can teach you something, even now."

I'm sure God can teach me something, but right now I'm a little ticked, I thought. *And anyway, what can I possibly learn from being hurt and having to quit Worlds again?*

I was upset, but I had given it my all, and I had been close to winning. It was light-years away from my Edmonton performance. Now every decathlete in the world knew I was a force to be reckoned with.

After the emotions subsided, I was pleased with how I had done. It was the first time on the international level that I had put myself in the spotlight, even if just for three or four events. I was proud of that and filled with determination about the upcoming Olympic year.

My 2003 season was done at that point. I had spent it gaining new knowledge about every event, taking my commitment to new levels, and internalizing the habits that were giving me success in life and on the track.

I also got a new manager, Paul Doyle. I met him over pizza in Paris. Rana introduced us, and Paul struck me instantly as someone I could work with. We've had a handshake agreement ever since. Before we left Paris, Paul got me my first shoe deal, with Nike, even though I hadn't even finished the meet.

> "There's a reason God takes you through a situation like this. He can teach you something, even now."

Kevin made me watch the rest of the World Championships from the stands again. Headed into the last events, Tom Pappas was leading, but Roman was nipping at his heels. With a big javelin throw, Roman could have passed him up. I watched as Roman came down the runway and launched the jav. It was a massive throw, 74 meters (242 feet 9 inches) or so, and the one he needed to win. But as he threw, he fell forward and landed on the ground in a push-up position. His finger just crossed the line and caused a foul. He didn't get a throw that big again.

Tom was vulnerable in the 1500, and Roman was speedy, able to run it in 4:20. The competition would be decided in the last event. Both men lined up, and Roman ran hard, but it wasn't enough. Tom hit the time he needed to win the meet, posting a final score of 8,750, just under his personal best. His reign continued.

As I watched the medal ceremony, I felt a steely certainty that I would be back. And next time I would win.

TEN
INCHES FROM THE GOLD

Nearly every time I talked with my mom, she repeated what she had been saying for years: she was praying for me daily, and I was going to win Olympic gold. She often pressed me, "Bryan, how are you feeling? Are you confident? How are you mentally? You know, you're going to make the Olympics and win the gold medal."

I tried to avoid these conversations because I didn't want to think about the Olympics yet. If I tried to say anything remotely discouraging about my chances, she stopped me: "Bryan, I don't want to hear any negative talk. You're going to win that medal. I'm praying for you." And that would be that.

In the meantime my relationship with Sarah had reached decision time. We had talked a lot about marriage, but it's safe to say I wanted more time to think about it than she did. Truth is, I was terrified of being married. My expectation was that as soon as we said, "I do," our relationship would transform from a romance into a war. The difficulties I had witnessed between my parents caused me to see marriage as an uphill battle, an unhappy experience that often ends in divorce. There were many divorced people among my family and friends. I feared divorce more than anything because it had hurt me so much.

Sarah anticipated no such problems. She said, "It's going to be so much fun! We're going to do this and that. Marriage is going to be great." To me, she seemed to live in fantasyland. I always took the opportunity to remind her that marriage would be a lot of work with many hard times, not the fun and games she predicted.

One day after I had popped her bubble again, she looked at me with wounded eyes and said, "Why does marriage always have to be so negative for you? All you say is how hard it is, how many rough times we're going to have. But marriage can be fun. It doesn't have to be all work." She had a point; I was being too negative because of my fears.

Still, I kept delaying and saying, "Let's make sure." Everything about me said it was time to get married, but I wondered whether I was ready to work that hard. Sarah had made up her mind. She brought it up every other weekend. And whenever we went out to dinner, she seemed to expect a ring and a formal proposal.

> I feared divorce more than anything because it had hurt me so much.

Her friends were getting married so that put even greater pressure on me. I begged off, saying, "Sarah, please trust that when I feel it's right, I'll propose. I want to marry you, but I want to wait until God tells me it's time." It was a classic excuse—I was blaming God for my inaction. But it wasn't about God; it was about me.

I had never told anyone, but I had several goals I wanted to achieve before I got married. Most of them were financial. One was to have

$10,000 in the bank. Another was to have my college degree. I wanted a car and no debt. I wanted to have an adequate income. In other words, I wanted to be a fully functioning adult before I got into a situation where I would, I hoped, be supporting a family.

With my career suddenly taking off, I also wondered whether getting married would interfere with my success. Friends and family warned me, "Don't get married. It will be a distraction. You won't perform as well as you could." Married people shared that the first five years were hard for them. As much as I loved Sarah and knew she was the only one for me, I thought that we might be wise to wait.

Finally I consulted Coach Barnett. I told him I was thinking of asking Sarah to marry me and needed some advice. What did he think about getting married so close to the Olympics? Would it get in the way of that opportunity? Was I a fool to even think about making such a big life change at such a promising time in my career?

Coach Barnett listened thoughtfully and then said, "Bry, as important as training and the Olympics are, you can't put your life on hold. There's no guarantee you'll make the team. If you put the rest of your life on hold that whole time, you're going to be a disappointed, unhappy person if you never make it. But if you live life and still train and don't let yourself get distracted, then you've got something to fall back on if the Olympics don't work out. Yes, the Olympics would be fun, but some things matter more."

Nobody else had told me that. Almost every other athlete I knew who was a serious competitor had pressed the pause button on everything else in his life. But I trusted Coach Barnett, and his advice made sense. I didn't want to wake up one day in my thirties and not have anything else going in my life except track. So I gathered my courage and asked Sarah's father if I could propose to his daughter. I had a good relationship with Sarah's family, but asking for her hand in marriage was the most nerve-racking moment of my life to that point. I opened my mouth a couple of times, and nothing came out. Finally I got the words out; to my relief, he readily agreed. I proposed to Sarah, and we were married January 2, 2004, at Sarah's childhood church in Seattle. By then I had met all my financial goals. It was as if God had knocked out the legs from under my remaining excuses.

The reality of marriage proved how wrong I had been to worry and how right Sarah had been that marriage could be fun. Instead of being a drain or a distraction, our marriage was, from the start, the biggest blessing of my life, aside from the Lord. It made me stronger on and off the track. It made me a better all-around person. It filled me with love and a sense of peace. I enjoyed coming home to Sarah after the end of a hard day at the track. The first year of our marriage, contrary to everyone's predictions, was the most amazing year I could imagine.

Being married also put me in a different situation from some of the other athletes at meets. They were partying and messing around with girls wherever they went. Decathletes are popular, especially in Europe, and have plenty of opportunity for temptation. I had heard wild stories of what happened there that scared me; I did not want to get pulled into that life. Things were going well for me, and I did not want to find myself in a situation where my character and ethics could be tested or questioned. I even prayed early on, "God, if I'm not strong enough to handle these temptations, please don't let me have success as an athlete. I would rather have Sarah than any gold medal."

> "As important as training and the Olympics are, you can't put your life on hold. . . . Some things matter more."

After I got married, I remained vigilant about protecting my honor and my relationship with Sarah. When I traveled, I almost always took someone with me—Sarah, a coach, or a friend. I always put two airline tickets in my contract. One time I took my pastor with me to a meet in Jamaica because my coaches and Sarah couldn't be there. The other athletes asked me, "You brought your pastor? What is wrong with you?" But my marriage is so important to me that I will do anything to protect it—even if I look foolish to some people.

Other athletes surely thought I was missing out on good times, but I knew better. I was happier than they would ever be doing what they were doing. When I overheard them talking about their sexual exploits in this or that city, I thought, *I'm so glad I'm married.* They might have had a temporary physical thrill, but real fun is having someone who loves you all the time. These guys went back to empty houses or to girlfriends whose commitment was questionable, especially after their careers were over. I had the privilege of going home to somebody who ultimately didn't care if I won or lost. She was always going to be there for me. She had committed to me for a lifetime and I to her. That reassurance gives me lasting joy.

The people who told me I should wait to get married were not only wrong but could have harmed my career. I never felt better, more energized, and more confident as an athlete than after Sarah was wearing that wedding ring. Getting married was one of the foundations for my future success.

Showdown in Sacramento

I took time off in August, as usual, after Worlds 2003 and started training at the end of September. It had taken a few weeks to heal from the hamstring injury, and I was already over what had happened in Paris. I make a habit of giving myself one day to be upset and sulk, and then it's over. Time to get back to work.

Fall training is like starting over with general preparation and conditioning. We do simple things to get my body ready to compete in six months. Track and field, like any sport, is cumulative. I can't just start competing full strength, or I will get injured pretty quickly. I have to build up strength and endurance over time. In the fall that means doing a lot of repetitions but not a lot of weight. It means working on the range of motion in my joints and tendons so I am flexible enough to take advantage of my speed and strength.

As the spring approaches, I slowly start pushing the envelope and building the intensity. At comp phase, or competition phase, the body is ready to perform at close to max, so I do exercises of more intensity and less volume: heavier weights with fewer repetitions, for example. At that point I am pushing myself to see what I can do.

A short recovery is built into the schedule every week, and a week-long recovery is scheduled every month. The idea is to take recovery when you want it, not when your body demands it. During recovery weeks, the workouts are lighter, and my body solidifies its gains. If I do all these things correctly, it's like a slow crescendo, and I peak at the right time.

> I make a habit of giving myself one day to be upset and sulk, and then it's over. Time to get back to work.

I was learning to trust the training program more and more. A young athlete easily can be either overconfident or underconfident. If overconfident he may think, *I had a great year last year. I'm going to crush the competition this year.* If underconfident he panics because he distrusts the program and may not be jumping as high or running as fast as expected. I had distrusted the program when I unilaterally quit doing weights back in my freshman and sophomore years of college.

But since then I had learned that if I train hard and believe in the program, I would avoid the two extremes. I was becoming mature enough to finally understand it all.

It is still common for me to have bouts of worry four weeks out from a meet because I don't feel that I trained enough and maybe I'm not running fast enough or throwing far enough. But the marks almost always arrive right on time for the big competitions.

We were living in a rented apartment near APU. Sarah was supporting us by teaching kindergarten. I was training full-time, and my small Nike endorsement was helping us a little bit financially. My goal was to do well in July at the Olympic Trials in Sacramento and make the team. It was a high goal, but I felt ready for it. From January to June I trained hard and competed mostly in individual events at track and field meets. The intensity was much different and higher for my coaches and me. They were putting their best advice and work and long hours into my training. I was putting pressure on myself because I knew there was no excuse for me not to win some of these big events.

I went to a meet in Estonia, my first one on the professional circuit and the first one to which I was invited and paid to compete. It was the first time I was listed as "Bryan Clay—Nike" rather than "Bryan Clay—Unattached." I had gone from an amateur to a pro, and that gave me an emotional and mental boost. I did okay and notched a score high enough to get an invitation to the IAAF World Indoor Championships in Budapest, which is by invitation only. There I placed second to Roman, and my score of 6,369 was the highest ever to get second place, and the second-highest score ever by an American in the heptathlon (Dan O'Brien had the highest).

It wasn't the last time I would post a gold-medal score only to have Roman snatch it away with an even better performance. He is an incredible competitor.

All year long I was watching my competition, keeping up with their marks, and studying their strengths and weaknesses. Because I was familiar with the other guys' stats, there were no surprises in a meet. I pretty much knew what they would do. The guys I was keeping up with most were Roman and Tom. Roman, a Czech citizen, wouldn't be at the USA Championships. But Tom would, and Tom was the guy to beat in 2004.

Tom is a big, strapping guy and a hard worker. Although he is from Oregon, he attended the University of Tennessee, and he set the collegiate record there. He is especially good in the shot put and high jump, but he is solid in everything. Anybody who wins a world championship has to be solid in everything. Like me, Tom is quiet and reserved, not a showboater. He tends to do his thing without drawing attention to himself. He is a respectful opponent and never talks trash about other athletes.

I had gone from an amateur to a pro, and that gave me an emotional and mental boost.

All the publicity in 2004 was about Tom because he had won Worlds the year before in Paris. He was without question the top decathlete in the United States. Everyone expected him to win the Trials and maybe even the Olympic Games. He was also a sympathetic favorite because he is of Greek heritage, and the Olympics were being held in Greece. The United States had put its hopes on him to bring decathlon gold back home. We had lost the title of world's greatest athlete in 2000, and Tom was the guy who would get it back.

By contrast, nobody mentioned my name. Few publications or observers picked me to medal at Trials. I was virtually invisible, a true underdog—and I loved it. I thrive in the second position. It helps me to get into my own world and do my routine without the distracting glare of the klieg lights.

Of course, Tom wasn't the only guy to beat. There were plenty of guys in the meet who had scored 8,200 or 8,300 points, and any of them could have a good meet and post a big score. I knew I could score 8,400, but even that was not certain. When we got to Sacramento, it was brutally hot—triple digits—like a convection oven on the track at Cal State Sacramento. Difficult conditions like that can throw some guys off their game, and I had to focus even more to keep the heat from affecting me.

I was grateful to have family there to watch the meet: my mom and stepdad, my grandparents, Sarah and her parents, my brother, and others. It was the first time my mom would see me finish a big meet. Someone had made up shirts that said, "Clay Ohana," and everyone wore them. It gave me an extra boost to know that a bunch of people I loved were in the stadium rooting for me.

On competition morning, July 16, I did my normal routine and watched the temperature climb fast. It felt hot at 8:00 a.m. All of us athletes had to manage the heat as well as our energy. I got into the meet and was so focused on my routines that I felt as if I had on blinders. Everything clicked, and I kept myself emotionally and physically cool. I could tell in my muscles and from my marks that I was crushing it from start to finish.

The result on day two was a score I had never achieved before: 8,600, 178 points more than my previous best. That put me fifth or sixth on the U.S. all-time list. I had personal bests in the discus (52.10 meters, nearly 171 feet), pole vault (5.10 meters, 16 feet 9 inches), and javelin (68.36 meters, 224 feet 3 inches). If I hadn't run the 1500 in a dismal 5:06 because of the heat, my score would have been even higher.

Not only that but I stunned the crowd and the national audience by beating Tom and winning my first major national meet. I was heading to the Olympics in Athens, Greece. The feeling was dreamlike. Having my head down for so long, working at my sport, then looking up and suddenly realizing I had arrived at a major goal was almost more than I could take in.

> I was virtually invisible, a true underdog—and I loved it.

My family was standing at the finish line, waiting for me to come over so they could congratulate me. I had draped myself in the Hawaii state flag and taken the victory lap with the other athletes, but before I could join my family, a television announcer grabbed me and wouldn't let me go. He kept saying, "Hang on. Hang on." I stood there waiting for him to interview me, and it took so long that I was getting frustrated.

Finally I heard him talking on his headset: "Oh, we didn't get any footage of the 1500? Okay, never mind." He walked away from me without another word. I thought, *I just won Trials and set a stadium record, and that's it?* He hadn't even apologized for holding me so long. To this day I avoid doing interviews with that guy. I usually let things slide, but he didn't seem to understand basic courtesy.

The fact that the network hadn't videotaped the final event of the decathlon only underlined the reality that dec takes place mostly out of the spotlight. You can't get too bigheaded when they don't bother to get footage of your climactic victory.

I went out to dinner with my family and had a great time. The next day the media started noticing me. The *Los Angeles Times* ran a story headlined "An Overlooked Star" and subheadlined "Many experts were surprised when Azusa Pacific's Clay won the decathlon at the Olympic trials." *Times* staff writer Mike Penner noted that

Track & Field News, which considered itself the "Bible of the sport," had virtually ignored my career at Azusa Pacific, where my decathlon scores would have made me the NCAA Division I champion for an unprecedented three consecutive years. Penner also mentioned that in recent months I had started putting up what the *Times* called "startling numbers."

The question for me and for decathlon observers was, could I put up enough "startling numbers" to make a splash in Athens?

Athens Bound

Back at APU after a day or two of rest, the intensity level went up again, and I trained as never before. I was about to go up against the best in the world for one of the most coveted medals in our sport. I couldn't show up slouching.

In my mind I was shooting for fifth place, which I thought would be an excellent showing for a twenty-four-year-old at his first Olympics. I thought if I could do that, I could build on it over the next four years and perhaps medal at the 2008 Olympics.

Within a few short weeks I was headed to Athens, where I shared a spartan dorm room with Tom Pappas. It didn't even have a television. I had arrived before my coaches and had nothing to do but sit there and feel my nerves jangle. I was happy when the opening ceremonies arrived to take my mind off competition. It was an amazing experience to stand outside the stadium with hundreds of other athletes, then walk down the concourse and hear the music and celebration as each country was announced. It felt like the Super Bowl. When the United States was introduced, the place went nuts, and we walked in wearing our team gear, waving, and watching the cameras flash like a thousand electric fireflies. It was an incomparable experience.

The next day the track and field team flew out to the island of Crete where our team had rented a resort. It was a phenomenal location, right on the beach. In the nearby town we found a restaurant and made friends with the owner, a big hairy shirtless guy with a pretty wife. He was also the cook. Every night we had Greek salads and meat skewers and the most wonderful time with each other and the owners. We ate there every day for two weeks, and I didn't want the whole experience to end.

> I was about to go up against the best in the world for one of the most coveted medals in our sport. I couldn't show up slouching.

My coaches met me in Crete, and my practices were outrageous. One particular high jump practice was beyond anything I had done before, and I jumped a personal best of 214 centimeters (7 feet), an inch and a half higher than what I had ever done in a meet. Long jump practices were great, and shot put was great. Everything was on. I had trusted the training regimen and was peaking at exactly the right time.

Two days before the decathlon started, we flew to Athens. We had rented a house for me, Rana, Kevin, Coach Barnett, Paul, and a couple of other temporary coaches. My dad and some of my aunts and uncles were staying elsewhere in Athens, which was wonderful because in a new city buzzing with anticipation, it's nice to have a familiar face and familiar feeling. Holding to their commitment to go to the Olympics if I made the team, the guys from my D-group had traveled all the way to Athens to cheer me on. Their support meant the world to me.

Sarah had not come because of the dangers still presented by terrorism. The U.S. Olympic Committee had told us they could protect athletes but not family members. Sarah and I had had a long discussion about it, and she and my mom had decided to stay in the States. It was my first Olympics, and if questions about their safety distracted me even in a small way, they would never forgive themselves. In the end, the fact that they were not there would be my only regret about the 2004 Olympics.

I woke up the first day at 5:00 a.m. and started my routine: a jog in the streets, oatmeal for breakfast, earphones in, no talking. I went to the track at 7:00 a.m. and walked around it once or twice, going through each event for that day in my head. I visualized myself burning through the 100, having a great long jump, a great high jump, a huge shot put, and a fast 400. Then I warmed up and went to the call room. I felt terrific.

Now and then the thought would intrude: *Wow. I'm at the Olympic Games. This is my dream.* Everything looked bigger than I expected: the track, the stadium, the massive crowd, even the sky above. I was excited to be wearing my Olympic gear. But I didn't dwell on those thoughts. I got right back to focusing on the next step. I tried to tell myself that it was just another meet, another World Championships, something to which I had already become accustomed.

I ran a terrific time of 10.44 in the 100, just shy of a personal best. Roman ran 10.85, the beginning of a great meet for him. Tom ran 10.80, which was okay but nothing special. We didn't know it at the time, but Tom was struggling with a foot injury that would keep him from scoring as high as he might have.

Everything was going just as I had hoped, but while I was warming up for the long jump, something unexpected intruded. I was going through my routine when the crowd got suddenly very loud, cheering and chanting *"Hellas,"* which means "Greece." I looked up at the screen and saw a Greek female race walker nearing the end of her race—and winning. The cheering, chanting, drums, and music were so deafening that I couldn't hear my coaches who were just a few feet away from me. I didn't have much choice but to stop my warm-up and watch the scene unfold.

The race walker on the screen suddenly emerged from the tunnel into the stadium. She had arrived for the final lap, and it was clear she was going to win. The emotion in that place exploded, and home-town Greek fans cried and hugged each other.

Almost without knowing what was happening to me, I was swept away with it. Overwhelmed, I started to cry. Their excitement and emotion were drawing out my suppressed excitement at living my dream. I tried to hide the tears behind my sunglasses, but every time I almost got a handle on it, I started weeping again. In moments I went from feeling serene and self-possessed to feeling emotionally out of control.

> Everything was going just as I had hoped, but while I was warming up for the long jump, something unexpected intruded.

The crowd kept whooping and applauding. I jogged back and forth, trying to shake it off, but it wasn't until the race was over and people settled down that I leveled out and got back into a routine. Before returning to the event, I got down on my knees and prayed, "Lord, thank You. If I win or lose or don't even finish the meet, thank You for this moment right now. It's what I have been dreaming about my entire life. Now let me do well."

I got up and put my thoughts on the long jump.

The first of my three jumps was okay, but I fouled, so it didn't count. I came back and did a second jump and the length was better, but I fouled again, this time by a millimeter or so.

Suddenly I was down to my last attempt. I looked over at my coaches; their faces were ashen. I was one misstep away from fouling out of the Olympics on my second event. For some reason I wasn't worried. I lined up, said a quick prayer, did my routine, counted my steps, ran down the runway, and launched.

I landed 7.96 meters (26 feet 1 inch) away, a decathlon personal best. But the official did not raise the white flag to signal a fair jump. He and the other officials walked over to inspect the Plasticine strip at the foul line to look for any evidence that I had stepped over the line. Usually the flag—red for foul, white for fair—goes up almost instantly. The longer it took, the more it seemed that they had found evidence of a foul. I stood there waiting. Every breath I took seemed to take minutes.

After agonizing moments, the white flag went up. Fair. My toe apparently had come within a millimeter of the foul line but did not cross it. I had turned in a peak performance on the most criti-cal jump of my life. My coaches exhaled and laughed nervously. I just gave them a look that said, *What were you so worried about?*

Tom jumped 7.38, which was poor for him, and at that point I realized that something was

> "Thank You for this moment right now. It's what I have been dreaming about my entire life."

wrong. He threw below his normal mark in the shot and jumped 2.03 in the high jump, several inches below his typical range. He found himself in fifth place. Roman threw a terrific 16.36 in the shot and had close to a personal best in the high jump. He was on pace to domi-nate, but somehow I was keeping up with him. I knew he was feeling pressure from my performances.

Before the last event of the day, the 400, I had to lie down for a while to rest. The Olympics have an intensity that is unique among all meets, and I felt mentally and physically weary. I needed to get away for a moment. My coaches told me I had ten minutes or so, and as soon as I lay down, I drifted off. It felt wonderful to let my mind go and feel my body relax, even for a short time. I was almost asleep when Kevin ran in.

"You're in second heat! You've got to go."

I sat up. "I'm not in the second heat," I said. "That's not what the schedule said."

"They changed the heats. Get up! We've got to go."

So many people had dropped out by then that the organizers were combining heats. That meant I had no time to warm up. Under the stadium was a practice track; on the way out, I sprinted down it twice, then had to immediately get in line and walk out for the race.

I had turned in a peak performance on the most critical jump of my life.

While we were walking, I stepped out of line and sprinted down the track 100 meters or so.

"No, no, no, you've got to come back," said one of the officials. Instead of warming up for twenty minutes, I had warmed up for maybe forty seconds. As they called my heat and I lined up to run, I still felt groggy. My head was back under the stadium catching some zs.

The gun went off, and I ran the first 200 as hard as I could, then came around the turn and had nothing left in my legs. I should have been pouring it on, but I fell back, unable to summon any reserves. Everybody, and I mean everybody, passed me on the last straightaway. I felt as if I was going to die. Roman ran a solid 48.36. Dmitri Karpov of Kazakhstan ran a blazing 46.81 and was clearly having the meet of his life. I ran 49.19, more than a second off what I should have done. I was still third behind Dmitri and Roman, but I had missed out on racking up some points.

It was an unfortunate thing to happen, but what could I do? It was a decathlon. Anything could happen, and for that event, it did.

"Don't Settle"

Day one ended on that ambiguous note, and I began the process of recovery. I was dehydrated, and the team doctor took me into a room with my coaches to give me an IV. For some reason he had trouble finding a vein. He kept poking me in search of one, and I noticed his hands were shaking. At one point my blood spurted all over the room. I'm not sure if he was nervous or what, but my coaches were very unhappy.

"What's going on?" Kevin barked. "This is ridiculous. Can we have our doctor do it?"

"No, I need to do it," the guy insisted. "I'm the team doctor."

It probably didn't help that my coaches were standing there, watching his every move. A nurse friend told me later that doctors rarely do IVs, so this guy was probably inexperienced at it, even if he was a good doctor. He eventually got it in, and without waiting I headed downstairs for an ice bath.

The ice bath was in a big trash can—the kind you probably wheel out to the curb every week—full of ice and water. I carefully climbed into the 50-degree water while Kevin held the IV bag above me and squeezed it to make the fluid go into me faster. Ice baths always hurt, especially my ankles and toes. After four minutes or so, my body went numb, and I relaxed as well as I could in such a situation, my body freezing and an IV sticking out of my arm.

Someone had been sent out to bring back dinner, but everything had closed down early in Athens. When the guy returned from his errand, he said, "The cafeteria was closing, so I grabbed what I could." He handed me a couple of toothpicks bearing tiny chunks of chicken, wrapped in a napkin. I thought my coaches were going to lose it.

"This is dinner?" they asked. "This is the best you could do?"

I started laughing at the whole scene. I had some protein shakes with me, so I drank those, ate the chicken miniskewers and four bananas, and drank two bottles of Gatorade. That was dinner.

I shivered the whole cab ride home and took a short hot shower to avoid diminishing the effects of the ice bath. At 2:00 a.m. I fell into bed thinking, *I wonder if I'm too wound up to go to sleep.* That was the last thing I remember.

The time to get up arrived so fast that I doubted there had been a night at all. It was 5:00 a.m. and I felt as if I had tumbled down a rocky mountainside. Under the blankets I moved my toes, then my ankles, then my legs. Every motion hurt. I rolled over, got out of bed on my hands and knees, felt the pain for a moment, somehow got dressed, and started my neuromuscular wake-up, which is a fancy term for jogging and running drills. I didn't even brush my teeth.

After that I had the luxury of sitting in a hot shower for half an hour, my eyes closed, basically asleep, sitting against the wall of the tub, and hoping the water wouldn't fill up my mouth and drown me. One of the coaches eventually knocked on the door and summoned me to breakfast.

I was so tired I couldn't imagine lifting a spoon, let alone hitting my marks in five different events. At that point I was still thinking 2004 would be my first Olympics, but not my last, and some conversation passed between my coaches and me about trying to do well here but really aiming for 2008. Coach Barnett seemed bothered by the discussion, and before we headed to the stadium, he pulled me aside and sat me down.

"Bryan, I have never told anyone this," he said. "But I think you need to hear it. My life goal was always to make the finals of the Olympic Games in javelin. I didn't go in wanting to medal. I just wanted to make the top eight and advance to the final round. When I got my shot, I was thirty-two years old. I had been training for thirteen years. I was working full time to support my family. I was right at the edge of being done with my athletic career. I got to Barcelona and competed, and I made the top eight and advanced to the final round. At that moment I had a sense of relief because I had achieved my goal, but I still wasn't done competing. I had three more throws. I had a shot at gold. But I remember smiling and thinking, *I did it.* I took those last three throws, but they didn't mean much to me. I had lost my competitive drive. I was satisfied."

He stopped for a moment to contain his emotion.

"You don't know how badly I wish I could take back those three throws. I wish I had given it my best rather than relaxed too early. The silver medal winner that year threw a distance that was shorter than my personal best. I could have medaled if I had focused. It took me years to realize I had given away a chance to be a champion. Only later did I understand that I had thrown away a once-in-a-lifetime opportunity that had taken me so long to obtain."

He looked me in the eyes.

"Bryan, don't assume you will get back here. Don't talk about 2008. This easily could be your last games. Don't settle. Don't give up on any throw, any jump, any race, no matter how tired you are. Treat this like the last time you will ever be in this position. Do your best, and you won't ever regret it."

Coach Barnett was right. I had been too cocky. The chance of making another team is always thin. Anything can get in the way. I thanked him, and as I went out that day, his words and the sense of regret he had shared stayed with me. I focused as never before, did my routines, hit my marks, and held nothing back.

Coach Barnett also told me something I think few athletes hear from their coaches: he was praying for me. He even said he had written down specific marks for this competition that had been on his heart. What they meant, he didn't know, but he made a record just in case. I realized again how nice it was to have coaches who didn't yell at me but prayed for me and encouraged me.

Record-breaking Results

When the competition started, I was still having a hard time concentrating for lack of sleep. It was going to be tough to turn in a world-class performance in my condition, and my only consolation was that the other athletes were feeling the same way. Being that sore, I'd lose range of motion, and run and jump and throw differently. There was no way to compensate for it. I went into the hurdles with one goal: *don't fall*. As long as I didn't fall, I would be in the hunt. A poor score was better than disqualification.

We lined up. I heard small grunts and groans and knew the other guys were feeling as drained as I was. My ears caught the sound of the gun. We broke off the line. One hurdle, two hurdles, three hurdles . . .

> It was going to be tough to turn in a world-class performance in my condition.

I was hitting each one with my back foot and mowing them down, but it wasn't hurting my speed too badly. I was staying upright and even winning the heat. So far, so good.

Then I crested the fourth hurdle, and my leg banged into it much harder, sending a shockwave through my body. I began to fall and stumble into the lane next to me. I had no time to think, only to react.

Listening to the live streaming Internet broadcast of the event in Hawaii, Sarah and my mom heard the announcer say, "And Bryan

Clay hit the fourth hurdle! He hit it hard. What a disaster for Clay!" Sarah started crying.

But somehow in that microsecond between the fourth and fifth hurdles, I righted myself and kept from going down. My speed was gone, but I was still in the race. I hit only the seventh hurdle after that and tried to accelerate to the end. My score: 14.13. A lot slower than usual. I didn't win the heat. I put my hands on the back of my head and walked out the disappointment. Then I slapped my legs in frustration and bent over to think it through. At least I hadn't gone down.

Sarah and my mom didn't realize I had finished the race until the radio announcer read the results. Only then did they know that my Olympic dreams were still alive.

Dmitri and Roman were having good meets, and the three of us were vying for the top spots. It almost seemed unreal. I had come to Athens hoping for a fifth-place finish; now I was in the top three. In the discus I threw 50.11, which was good, but Dmitri threw 51.65. Roman threw a decent 48.72. Dmitri remained in second place even though I outjumped him in the pole vault. Then I hurled the javelin for a personal best 69.71 meters (228 feet 8.5 inches), and the huge point swing put me in second. The crowd was with me, and I could feel it. But I was so tired; I just wanted to lie down and let the meet end. Had I allowed myself to go to sleep, I don't think a jet engine would have awakened me.

When it was time to run the 1500, I went out and ran as hard as I could, crossing the finish line in 4:41.65, one of my best times ever in that event. As I caught my breath, I looked up at the board to see what nobody expected: a monster score of 8,820 beside my name. That put me second all-time on the U.S. list (again behind Dan O'Brien). If I had run the 1500 a hair faster, I would have become the highest-scoring American ever.

In any other year, 8,820 would easily have been good enough for gold. But this was no ordinary year. My new nemesis, Roman Sebrle, had showed unbelievable grit and athletic ability, digging deep and setting an Olympic record to fend me off. I missed gold by 73 points, a whisker. Athens was the highest-scoring decathlon in history, and my point total remains the highest ever for a silver medal.

What I had achieved was so far above my coaches' and my expectations that I couldn't be disappointed. I beat out some incredible athletes, Dean Macey, Tom Pappas, and Erki Nool among them. As I stood on the podium that night, the silver medal around my neck, I almost felt as if I had stepped into another person's reality. How had I gotten here? Yes, I had trained hard and devoted my career to this. But so do thousands of other people.

God had made the difference. His presence, His wisdom, His principles, and His love had filled my life and elevated it in every way. Now here I was, one of the top two decathletes in the world and in American sports history. My heart was flooded with gratitude to God, to my coaches, to my family. Team Clay had come up big.

> **What I had achieved was so far above my coaches' and my expectations that I couldn't be disappointed.**

That evening Coach Barnett approached me and put his arm around my neck. "Remember those marks I told you I wrote down?" he asked. "We hit every one of them."

We looked at each other and marveled for a moment. All I could say was, "Wow!" There wasn't really anything else to add.

My only disappointment about Athens was that Sarah and Mom had not been there to share the greatest moment yet in my career. They are without question my two biggest fans. In spite of the terrorist threat, I regretted my decision to ask them to stay home. My experience there was priceless and, for all I knew, my high point in sports.

After I returned home from Athens, I told Sarah, "I don't care what it takes. If I make the next Olympic team, you are going to be there. I don't care if we spend our entire savings. I don't want to do it without you."

I felt especially strongly about it because I knew a big part of my doing so well in 2004 was being married and having a stable partner in my life. Sarah helped me settle down, focus, and stay grounded during the journey. One of the primary reasons I can do what I do on the track is that I have her. She's a rock.

Athens marked the beginning of my friendship with Roman. We had gotten acquainted in Paris, but in Athens we got to know each other personally. Our friendship flourished over the next four years even as we went head-to-head in some of the most intense battles the decathlon had ever seen.

Back home the *Los Angeles Times* (August 25, 2004) ran a nice article: "Clay Makes His Effort Stick." Helene Elliott wrote, "The silver medal [Clay] won Tuesday at the Summer Games should silence any remaining doubts about his ability or the power in his 5-foot-11, 174-pound body."

I had tasted success. I knew I was good enough to compete with anyone. Now I wanted to let people know that I could be the best. I joked with my coaches on the way home that if I had won gold, I probably would have retired. The truth was that if Roman had scored slightly lower on just one event or made a mistake, or if I had made one less mistake, my national anthem would have been playing that night.

I was capable of winning gold, and for the first time in my life, I believed what my mother had said all those years. She was confident I *would* win while I was confident only that I *could* if things turned out right. Anything can happen—injury, a cramp in a race, the rise of a talented new decathlete, or someone else having a phenomenal day. Those were things I couldn't control. But brimming with possibilities, my mind raced ahead to 2008. Everything I did from that point on was focused on Beijing.

Athens was a dream come true but not the whole dream. I was hungry for the gold.

ELEVEN
EMBRACING FATHERHOOD

Marriage was good to me from the very beginning, and within weeks of my returning from the Olympics, Sarah and I received more good news: she was expecting our first child. We were overjoyed. Both of us wanted kids right away, and now we would step into our dream of being parents.

Learning that I would be a father signaled a life shift as momentous as marriage had been. As I trained that fall, I spent a lot of time reflecting on what being a father meant. Though having children was something I wanted most in life, I was also a little afraid at the prospect of becoming a father. The responsibility seemed potentially overwhelming, and on a practical level I wasn't sure how to do it.

My view of fatherhood, as with much in my young life, was colored by my parents' difficulties and my difficulties with my stepfather before we found a good relationship. I began to research fatherhood and talk about it with friends.

One of the most important resources I found was the book *The*

Way of the Wild Heart by John Eldredge. It touched me deeply and taught me about boyhood and manhood. I read about the masculine journey and its different stages: cowboy, lover, warrior, king, and sage. Each stage seemed so important to me, and I realized that I had skipped some of them due to the transition from having a father and mother at home, to having just a mother at home, to having a stepfather whose authority I initially rejected. I was like many men who miss significant stages of growth for different reasons—no family situation is perfect.

As I had done on the track, I began to break down the problem into components and analyze each one. Why was I feeling the way I did? What specifically were my doubts? How did these threaten my dreams of being a father? What would perfect fatherhood look like? Where had I seen such fatherhood on display?

As I pondered my experience, I began to see that God had put many models of fatherhood in my life at key times. These examples gave me much to draw on as I pieced together the portrait of the father I wanted to be.

Footprints to Follow

My real dad was and is the most important earthly father I have. He remains my model for fatherhood and embodies much of what I want to be as a dad. My dad showed me strength, joy, and love, and those memories shine brighter with time.

One of the little things that still impresses me was his insistence on having peace at the dinner table, even during the family's hardest times. No fighting was allowed there. Everything stopped, and for that span of time we were a family. That taught me an important lesson: even in a time of trouble, you can choose peace. You can change direction. As a father, you can set the mood of the household.

My dad also showed me the importance of just being present for your children so they can observe you and talk with you and receive the wordless guidance that comes through example. He taught me how important it is for a child to hear that his father loves him and to show it in real ways, as my dad had shown us so many times by telling us he loved us. Following the divorce, he went out of his way to come to the bus stop near our playground to talk with me so we could spend precious moments together, which I still treasure.

When I think of a father, I picture my dad as a young man, the one who was and is my hero. I am thankful that we still have a great relationship today.

Before and following my parents' divorce, my grandfather was a strong fatherly presence in my life. In him I saw the strong leadership that grandfathers can give to an extended family. I also saw how the pursuit of perfect work paid off financially and in the satisfaction of a job well done. He was generous, as God is. He was demanding, as God is demanding of those who follow Him. The days I worked alongside him in his many business ventures indelibly imprinted those lessons on my mind. As I've said, the way I approach training and competition with such attention to detail, perfecting the little things, is a direct result of watching my grandfather work.

My real dad was and is the most important earthly father I have.

Mr. Awa, my sixth grade PE teacher, was another fatherly presence in my life. I realized that though his influence boiled down to a single incident, its impact on me was so powerful that it shaped my outlook on life. Mr. Awa had loved me in a way he no doubt found difficult. He had loved me enough to teach me a foundational lesson: Success is not just about raw talent. Success is about working hard and doing everything required of you. If Mr. Awa had given me a passing grade, allowing me to move on to the next grade, I would have missed that lesson and had to learn it somewhere else. If I had not learned it at all, I would not have succeeded in track.

From that experience I also learned that being corrected and gaining wisdom can be painful. Now when I am learning a hard lesson, I look back on my experience with Mr. Awa and know that along with the pain comes a greater level of maturity.

Richard Ainsworth also was an important father figure to me. When I was going through perhaps my darkest time as an adolescent, he embodied the peace and patience of God. Being with Richard taught me that many problems can be solved without words. You really need only the presence of God to calm your heart and help you see your way forward. At other times Richard took me in like a runaway or a prodigal, modeling the faithful love of God even toward those who persist in doing wrong. That's what Richard provided for me, by God's grace. Without him I'm sure I would have spun further out of control.

As I got older, my stepdad became an important father to me, and I appreciate what he did for my brother and me. He stepped into a messy situation and refused to give up. He knew love was a choice, not a feeling. He chose to love me when I gave him every reason not to. When I think back on the hard times we had, I am humbled by his example. He was a better man than I was. He was faithful, as God is faithful. Not once did he even threaten to walk out on our family. He was always there in the role of a father, providing for us, making rules so we had structure, and loving us.

My stepdad would take my brother and me out in his sailboat, and the three of us would spend the day on the ocean, out of Haleiwa Harbor on the north shore. We would have quiet times together, no reason or desire to argue or bicker. It was as if we all had called a truce. That's when I knew, looking out at the ocean and the horizon, that everything would be okay. He provided that for me.

I am ashamed now when I think about how I mouthed off to him and did everything I could to ignore and disrespect him, yet he still went out and bought me shoes and food and paid for me to join the club track team. Even when I ran away, he was always right there when I got home, and he never rejected me. My stepdad gave me what I needed: an authority figure, a roof over my head, and acceptance when I was at my worst. I am still grateful to him.

Mr. Hee was another father to me. His patience and dedication went far beyond what a typical teacher or coach provides. He loved me by investing his time and wisdom in me even when I quit the team. He had faith that I could have a career in sports long before I did. He saw my future—college with a scholarship—perhaps before anyone, except my mom. He was a quiet visionary and a loving authority figure. Among the many people in my *ohana*, I hold the Hees close to my heart.

> Success is about working hard and doing everything required of you.

While I was in college, Terry Franson became an important mentor for me. During a time in my life when I didn't know how to live right and was in a mini-depression because of Sarah's rejection of me and my lifestyle, I chose Terry. He seemed to embody the idea of a disciple, and that's what I wanted to become.

Terry did a lot to show me what being a Christ follower looked like in real life. I remember hearing his testimony in chapel and thinking, *This is one guy I don't think I could lie to.* He was known for loving his family, putting God first, and being very successful in the field of athletics. Those were the three things I wanted people to say about me. In Terry, God gave me a living, breathing, walking example of what my life could look like if I made the right choices. I saw him almost daily on campus and watched how he interacted with people. I wanted to literally follow Terry around so I could emulate his actions, words, and character. I wanted to follow him in the same way he followed Christ.

Terry also taught me a seemingly small but very important lesson. When I had asked if he would mentor me, he didn't immediately say yes. He said, "Let me take a day or two to pray about it." At the time I was taken aback. I did not understand why he couldn't make the decision right then and there. But he gave me a valuable decision-making tool. Instead of making snap decisions, he consulted God. I decided to try out that tool in my life, and I even used his line: "Let me take some time to pray about it." As I did, I realized that God wants to partner with me in my decisions. Sometimes my mind completely changed after I prayed about a decision. Terry taught me to talk to God about matters big and small. As the Bible says, "In all your ways acknowledge Him, and He shall direct your paths" (Proverbs 3:6 NKJV).

> My stepdad . . . knew love was a choice, not a feeling. He chose to love me when I gave him every reason not to.

The next father in my life was my father-in-law, Sarah's dad. I heard a lot about him from her when we were dating, long before I met him. She talked about the things they did when she was young: going on date nights, taking long bike rides, doing so many things together as a family. She would tell me about the hunting and fishing trips he took with his son. The guy seemed almost too good to be true.

He wasn't. From the moment we met I could see he was everything

Sarah had described. He treated me as his own son from the start. He took me hunting and fishing in Washington where he lived with his family. We also went on a trip together to Alaska and stood on the edge of the Kenai River, fishing and not really saying much. It called to mind those precious times with my stepfather and Richard Ainsworth, quietly enjoying nature together. I knew then that this was yet another relationship that God would use to teach me about being a man and a father. I have since made a side career of watching the way he treats his wife and children; it is how I want to treat mine. His example continues to shape my view of fatherhood and marriage.

Best of all I enjoy just sitting and talking with him over coffee. He'll tell me, "You did a good job. I'm proud of you." Those words mean the world to me. Like any young man, I like more than anything to have an older man say that I have done well. I have always treasured those relationships with older men who can give me wisdom and reassurance and who can answer my questions about life, faith, and all sorts of things. I am constantly seeking mentors I can talk to over breakfast or coffee and ask, "Have you thought about it this way? What about this?" Those conversations build up my life.

Going through this time of introspection and assessment before our son, Jacob, was born was just as important as my athletic training. It set me up to be the father I wanted to be. Most important, I saw how the combined examples of all these men in my life pointed me to my heavenly Father. Other people can be fatherly figures for a time, but they are put there by God to reflect His character.

As a result of all this personal study and observation, my relationship with God changed. Instead of seeing Him as authoritarian or rules oriented, I began to see Him as relational. I began to converse with God, to go back and forth, even to get upset and show emotion and not worry that He would negatively react to me. My relationship with Him became so much more meaningful and life-giving than I had ever imagined it could be. God loves me. He is committed to me. He is waiting to give good things to me if I seek Him. He still is my ultimate authority, but like the best fathers, He is also patient and understanding.

As the date approached for the birth of our first child, I went from a place of doubt and concern to a place of hope and thankfulness about what I would be like as a father. All I had to do was look in the direction of Christ and at the godly examples He had given me in the many fathers in my life.

TWELVE
AT THE TOP OF MY GAME

Competing in other meets after you have been in the Olympics is disappointing. Your sport goes back to being obscure. The eyes of the world look elsewhere. The scale of meets is so much smaller, the excitement so much lower. Everything seems ordinary.

I knew better than to expect anything to match the atmosphere of the games, but it was still a letdown to head to everyday meets in 2005 and think, *What am I doing here? Where's the energy?* It felt like graduating from college and then reenrolling in high school. On a personal level I was pumped and ready to go—I had new confidence and hunger to win—but my sport had shrunk back to size.

What kept me going was my goal: Olympic gold. Now it wasn't just my mom telling me I would win; I knew that gold could be mine, and preparing for the 2008 Olympics consumed me. Four years is a long time to focus on something, so I did as I usually did and put my sights on the ground ahead of me, taking it one small step at a time.

In 2005, my new friend and competitor Roman came to California to train with me. It may sound strange that the guy who beat me at the Olympics would want to spend time with me, but training with your competition is pretty common in the decathlon. For my part, I knew it was never a bad idea to train with the best decathlete in the world. For Roman's part, he wanted someone to push him. At that level it is hard to find people who can challenge you on your marks, so Roman and I naturally gravitated toward each other. We both wanted to deepen our friendship and improve our scores.

We trained at APU daily for three weeks. I pushed myself more than normal in practice to prove that I could keep up with him. The cool thing was that I found myself beating his marks in certain events, and day by day this superman—considered by many to be the perfect athlete—came down to size. Every little "win" was like a notch in my belt and made me more confident.

By the time Roman left I knew I could beat him in competition. Training together had humanized him in my eyes. The key to understanding any decathlete is knowing what he can do in practice because that is what he will consistently do in a meet. I had seen up close what Roman could do. I felt physically capable of outscoring him, but could I put together ten events in a real-world situation, a meet? Was I consistent enough? Those were my lingering questions.

I did not know it at the time, but winning Olympic gold is hugely draining, and Roman was probably in his post-Olympics funk. After expending yourself on such a big competition on such a huge stage, you just want a break, but you can't get one. The spotlight is on you, and you have to keep competing and responding to media requests. Your training suffers. You want to hide away and be alone, which is perhaps why Roman wanted to train with me in the first place— to return to the simplicity of the sport far away from the noise he encountered everywhere in Europe.

Off the track our friendship deepened, too, and later that year I went to the Czech Republic with my family and spent time with Roman and his family. We had a wonderful visit. Roman is a genuine person. He does not try to impress anyone with his accolades. He loves his wife and family, and he loves track and field; so many of our priorities are the same. When we are together, we don't try to impress each other. We just have a good time. We can also compete without ruining our friendship. We respect each other. In fact, if I don't win, I always hope Roman does.

Family vs. Competition

The rest of 2005 demonstrated two recurring themes in my life: the ability to win big and the ever-present danger of burning out.

Training and competing so hard in 2004 had left my body feeling broken down. I had nagging injuries that would not heal. So as 2005 began, my training at times felt lackluster. There were days when I wanted to do anything but go to the track. I did as I normally did and pushed through it, but in the back of my mind I wondered whether I would even make it through the season. Having put my attention so much on the sport in 2004, I just wanted to be home for a while and spend time with Sarah as we prepared for our first child.

At one point it looked as if the birth of that child would come into direct conflict with my competition schedule. The baby's due date was July 1, just one week after the USA Championships. To my great relief, the Championships were being held in Carson, California, at the Home Depot Center, not far from where we lived. But what would I do if Sarah went into labor while I was competing? Walk off the track and drop out of the meet? Or possibly miss the birth of my first child?

To me, the answer was clear: family first. I was not going to mess with the order of priorities that had made my life so much better. I was not about to elevate sports above my own child. Coach Barnett's advice was still good: Live life. Don't put everything on hold. I knew that God's plans for me went beyond track. God first, family second, track third. That's how it would stay.

My coaches wholeheartedly endorsed the decision, though none of us wanted it to come to that. So we put together a plan. Sarah's parents would be there. If she went into labor, they would take her to the hospital. If I could squeeze in a couple more events, I would. If not, I would leave. Having worked out the logistics as best we could, we prayed and put it in God's hands, believing that if it was meant to be, He would make it work.

The first day of competition brought 100-degree heat, and there was my very pregnant wife sitting in the sun at the Home Depot Center. I kept reminding her not to walk around so much. She was already dilated a few centimeters, and the doctor had told us the baby could come at any moment. I got her into a VIP area under a tent where she could watch the meet in the shade. Food and water were available there too. She and her parents were excited to watch me compete, yet I had to ask myself, *Would I have any jitters from the excitement of the impending birth?*

The Home Depot Center is great for track and field because the winds often blow strong. A wind coming at you can hold the discus up. It is no coincidence that my two best marks in discus were made there. It also has a nice track.

The competition opened with strong winds against us in the 100, which slowed down everyone's time. I ran it in 10.70 seconds. But the same wind held our discs up longer, making for higher scores. I threw 55.87 meters (183 feet 4 inches), setting a decathlon world record that stands today.

I managed to keep my focus pretty well—with no jitters—though occasionally I glanced up at Sarah to see how she was doing. By the end of day two, it was clear; I would not only win but win big. It was one of those meets where I said to my coaches, "Do I have to run the 1500?" I knew what the answer would be, but it was worth a shot. I loped across the finish line and won with a score of 8,506, more than 500 points ahead of second place.

I went home with the gold medal around my neck, marveling at the success that God was giving me. Jacob was born a week later, on July 1, 2005. The joy I felt holding that baby boy far outshone the joy I have ever felt at winning a meet.

Crazy Conditions

The World Outdoor Championships had always bedeviled me—I had never even finished one, let alone medaled. In August I traveled to Helsinki for Worlds, the culminating event of the year, wondering whether it would get the best of me again. The burst of enjoyment I had experienced at Carson faded, my body felt wrecked, and my mind was on home, on Jacob, and on being a father.

I flew alone to Finland, and for the first few days I mostly stayed in my hotel while waiting for my coaches to arrive. It was pouring rain, and the forecast called for only more. As the rain came down relentlessly, my mood sagged further. One night I called Sarah and told her, "I just don't want to be here. I wish I could get on a plane and come home. I don't even feel in good enough mental shape to compete."

"You can't come home," she said in tears. "You're already there. Your coaches are on the way. Just do the meet. Maybe they'll cancel it for weather."

She was even more concerned than I was that having a new child would distract me. She could tell I was in another place mentally, and she did not want family life to get in the way of my career.

The lesson I had learned about commitment was perhaps the only thing that kept me there. I stayed in Helsinki and fought through the mental battles. Soon I found myself at the track on day one of the meet. It was windy and raining sideways, the temperature a chilly 50-something degrees. At one point the rain came down so hard that the judges did something I had never seen them do—stopped the meet during the high jump because of the water accumulation on the track.

The athletes stood under the stadium, glumly watching it pour and knowing that the more it was delayed, the less time we had that night to recuperate. At one point a female U.S. hurdler tried to organize a boycott among all the female hurdlers: "If we all say we won't run, we can get the meet delayed. Who's with me?" Nobody took her offer. Nobody wanted to compete in the cold rain, but nobody was willing to bow out.

The meet began inauspiciously with Dmitri Karpov, the Athens bronze medalist, false starting out of the competition, a very rare thing for any decathlete to do. He jumped off the line early twice on the 100, and just like that, his day, his meet, and his season were over. All the other athletes were a little envious that he was going home. As I watched their reactions, I thought, *Everybody here is falling apart. Nobody wants to be here. Who knows? Maybe I'll do well. At least I'll go out and have fun.*

I thought back to when I was a seventh grader, running in the sugarcane fields of Hawaii, the rain pouring down and mud caked up to the top of my shoes. There was so much mud one day that one of my shoes actually came off because it was so heavy. I stopped to put it back on, then instead flipped off the other one and ran the rest of the race barefoot.

In the rain all you can do is give your best and let the results be. There was a massive 3.2 meters-per-second tailwind in the 100, and I ran 10.43, which disappointed me. With that smoking wind behind me, I thought I had run 10.1. I won the event, but I could not help wondering whether something was wrong with my legs.

The lesson I had learned about commitment was perhaps the only thing that kept me there.

The long jump went fine, and then came the shot. I got into the ring and did some warm-ups, lofting the shot from a finished position without taking a glide. It flew so far that I thought it might be a fluke. I threw it again, without any glide, and it flew just as far.

I'm feeling good, I thought. *Better not waste it in warm-up.*

I sat back down and waited. Sometimes you warm up great and do terrible when it really counts, so I couldn't get too excited about the long practice throws.

The rain was throwing a lot of guys off. It had erased the margin for error. Technically, rain should not affect performance at all. Spiked shoes keep you from slipping, and if your form in the jumps and throws is correct, the rain simply doesn't matter. But get off just a little in any of the events and the rain would magnify the error. Hit the ground with, say, your heel or the side of your foot while running the 100 or the hurdles and you might wipe out on the wet surface. Get off balance in the throwing or jumping events, which are more technical than the running events, and things could go wrong quickly because of the wet ring and unpredictable winds.

The fact remained, however, that if you performed technically close to perfect, the rain would not matter at all. Instead of imagining the consequences of failure, I focused on having perfect technique. That allowed me to forget about the rain.

Some guys had run tentatively in the 100 and in their long jump approaches, and in the shot they were slipping all over the place. Some took their socks off and slid them over their shoes inside out to gain a little more traction on the concrete. Each guy took a towel into the ring and sopped up the water just before his throw, even though the constant rain dampened the ring almost instantly. The officials used towels to dry the ring too.

When my turn came, the rain stopped briefly. I wiped up as much water as I could and quickly got into position for my first throw. I began my glide and missed the rhythm a bit, but the shot still flew surprisingly far. I tried not to get too excited about it. I looked over at Coach Barnett in the stands, and he signaled a couple of corrections for me to make in my movements. When it was my turn again, I lined up and took another throw, putting some heat on this one, throwing the shot as hard as I could. It traveled a meter farther than I had ever thrown before, a decathlon personal best. It remained my decathlon personal best until three years later when I beat it by 2 centimeters (less than an inch) on a much bigger stage.

My confidence was up, and the next day I knew the discus would be good. I got one throw in during a break in the clouds before it got nasty again. That throw was huge, 53.68 meters (176 feet 1 inch), 7 feet less than I had thrown in Carson but well ahead of the other competitors.

Rain? What rain?

Roman was having a good meet, too, and he pulled ahead after four events. But I came back in the 400 to regain the lead.

On day two the rain was just as bad. We ran into a headwind in the hurdles, which caused a lot of guys to plow over them like a harvester mowing down a field of wheat. The pole vault was almost comical. The pit was full of water, and whenever someone landed, the water splashed up so you could barely see the athlete. We all kept our poles under the tent, wrapped in towels. Each of us waited to go to the runway until the last possible second, then dashed out, the pole still wrapped in a towel. The procedure that seemed to work was to set our grips on the pole under the dry towel, let the towel go, and hold that grip so it remained dry.

The wind was blowing so hard that it affected us up top too. I remember running down, putting the pole in the box, and hanging on for dear life, hoping my grip wouldn't slip, hoping the pole would stay in the box, and hoping the wind would not blow me backward at the apex. All of us left that event soaked to the skin.

Through it all I kept turning in eye-popping scores for the conditions: a personal best

Instead of imagining the consequences of failure, I focused on having perfect technique.

of 47.78 in the 400, and a personal best of 72 meters (236 feet 2.5 inches) in the javelin, 2 or 3 meters more than I had ever thrown in competition. Somehow in those unlikely circumstances, I ran up a score of 8,732 points, winning by the largest point margin in World Championships history, 211 points.

I can't explain how it happened except that I had ignored the weather and relaxed because it was all so ridiculous. As I stood on the podium, received the medal, and listened to my anthem playing, I could hardly believe that just forty-eight hours earlier I had seriously considered hopping a plane back home. Not only had I won and banished the memory of Edmonton and Paris, but I had beaten Roman, which was a personal goal. He still seemed tired and in need of a break from the world scene. That was probably the only reason he didn't put up stiffer competition.

Scoring so big in such bad weather was a major confidence booster for me. On the flight home I wondered how much bigger my score might have been in good weather. Even though I had been to the Olympics and been competing at a high level for four years, Helsinki helped me to finally understand the power of believing I could win.

When I got home, Sarah just smiled and shook her head. We were both thinking the same thing: *It's a good thing you didn't come home.*

Leading the Pack

I went into 2006 as the top-ranked decathlete in the world. I was being called one of the best sprinter-hurdlers in the sport, one of the best jumpers, and one of the best-throwing decathletes ever to compete. I now held the world decathlon record in discus. In pole vault I was up to just shy of 17 feet, as good as any decathlete. That year I would high jump 210 centimeters (6 feet 10.5 inches), another personal best.

My confidence was high, and the work my coaches and I were putting in was paying off bigger than any of us probably expected. But that year would show me again that you never know what will happen on the day of competition. Success is never guaranteed.

At the 2006 IAAF World Indoor Championships, I should have won the heptathlon, but both Roman and I had embarrassingly sloppy meets. Things just went sideways for me in a bunch of events. I threw the shot horribly because I was experimenting with spinning rather than gliding, and it wasn't working out. In practice I had done fairly well with the spin, but I had practiced on concrete, which is slower than the painted wood rings used in indoor competitions. That ring threw everything off: my balance, my form, my technique. I had a couple of good events, but mostly the meet was a train wreck.

Nevertheless, I was awarded silver and Roman the bronze. While waiting to receive our medals, Roman leaned over to me and said, "I hate losing. If I lose to you, it's one thing, but anybody else, I hate it."

"Same for me," I said. "I'm all right losing to you, but we're better than this guy."

We both looked at the German on the top podium who was beaming ear to ear, having just beaten the two highest-ranked decathletes in the world. Roman and I shared a disgusted look. We had given him the meet. It was one of the lowest winning scores in Indoor World Championship history. I never had felt bitter about a medal before, but I did with that silver. To me it represented a botched opportunity. I was fine losing to someone who beat me when I was at my best. But we had given that one away.

Success is never guaranteed.

The outdoor season got off to a better start at the Hypo-Meet in Gotzis. Ask any decathlete: Gotzis is one of the best meets in the world. Imagine having the most enthusiastic and knowledgeable decathlon fans in the world, all in a beautiful Austrian mountain town near the Alps, with a beautiful and quaint track, music, food, and a great schedule. That's Gotzis.

The locals are amazing. They know each athlete and his marks. They gather on the grassy hillsides surrounding the track and cheer. There is even a big parade and ceremony for the athletes.

Best of all, instead of starting at 9:00 a.m. we start at noon. What a difference it makes to wake up naturally rather than to an alarm at 5:00 a.m. The whole thing is well organized and well run. The athletes also put on a minicamp for local kids to teach them about each of the events and take them through warm-ups.

Sarah and Jacob accompanied me, and I had a great meet, winning with a score of 8,677, which was 384 points ahead of second place, the biggest winning margin in the history of the meet. Roman withdrew on day one with muscle trouble. I won four events—the

100 in 10.42 seconds, long jump with 7.67 meters, hurdles with a personal best of 13.74 seconds, and the javelin with 66.47 meters. Dmitri Karpov was second with 8,293 points, and Maurice Smith of Jamaica finished third with 8,269.

That turned out to be the only decathlon I finished in 2006.

I caught some sort of cold right before the USA Outdoor Championships in Indianapolis and was taking over-the-counter medications when I arrived. Practices were still going well, so I thought I was on the upswing. My performance, though, soon showed otherwise.

I ran okay in the 100, but as I jogged it off, something felt funny inside. By the time I was warming up for the long jump, I felt nauseated. I lay down as long as I could and had to force myself to get up so I could get my step down. After a couple of runs I lay back down again even though I did not have my step figured out. I jumped poorly, 7.22 meters, and slept between events.

My coaches encouraged me to eat something, so I got a banana down, but it didn't help. My shot put was decent, 15.60 meters, and my high jump was a solid-but-not-great 202 centimeters.

Then it all fell apart in the 400.

I ran 48.15, a pretty good time, but did not remember half the race. I was dizzy, queasy, and starting to black out while running. My coaches and the officials saw I was about to fall over, and they carried me off the track to the medical tent. Everything kept fading in and out. They took my blood pressure and gave me at least two IVs. The diagnosis: severe dehydration and lack of nutrients. The illness and medications had done a number on me.

I went back to my room and tried to rest, but I had taken my body to the point of no return. It was depleted and would not recover quickly enough to compete. I tried to make it work on day two, but I couldn't even feel my legs during the hurdles. Discus came easy, so throwing 51.06 meters wasn't a problem. But in pole vault I could not get myself down the runway without feeling as if I would collapse at the end. I ran down three times but did not have the confidence to put the pole in the box. I no-heighted, and that was the end of the season for me.

I had done my best to finish, but no matter how hard I tried, I could not push through the illness. To keep going, I risked injury and lasting damage to my body.

At least I had emptied my tank trying.

Setback

The next year started with high excitement: Katherine Joy Clay was born February 2, 2007. Our family was growing, Sarah loved being a mother, and I was having the time of my life as a dad. I had never known such joy, such pride, such love. I thanked God daily for the amazing privilege of being a father and having such a wonderful wife and kids.

On the track my results were still spotty. In Gotzis I had a massive score going then inexplicably blew the discus. The announcer kept saying I was on pace to set an American record or even a world record. But two of my discus throws went out of the sector, and one slipped out of my hand for a final distance of 36.14, a ridiculous 40 feet short of what I usually did. I was so disappointed and dejected that I considered dropping out of the meet. Seven decathlons in a row I had thrown 50 meters (164 feet) or farther, and in an eighth I had thrown 49.88. I could not believe I had failed on one of my strongest events.

But commitment was a real thing to me, and I was not going to quit just because I was disappointed. The principles God had taught me continued to guide me, and I stuck with the meet, finishing at 8,493. I had to be happy, considering I had done it on the strength of nine events. It was enough for third place behind Andrei Krauchanka and Roman.

My body continued to show signs of wear, and I suffered from a lot of little nagging injuries, including ones to my elbow and shoulder that would not heal completely. If I finished a meet, I usually won it, including the World Indoor Championships, but I was not dominating as I had before. At the USA Championships, again held in Indianapolis, I had to drop out, this time because of a knee that kept swelling whenever I ran.

> I thanked God daily for the amazing privilege of being a father and having such a wonderful wife and kids.

Tom Pappas won with a score of 8,352. He was typically gracious and told the media that my presence was missed and that had I stayed in the competition it would have pushed his score higher. Tom had been bothered by injuries for so long that I was happy to see him back in top form.

I qualified by automatic berth for the 2007 World Championships in Osaka, and I was hoping it would redeem the year for me. I have strong family connections to Japan, so we made plans to go together, my mom and grandparents, Sarah and her family. I even thought I might have a little home-field advantage if the crowd got behind me.

The trip to Japan was a big deal for my grandparents, who were able to renew family relationships. I never had seen two people prouder of me, and for a while I felt like a showpiece. I was happy for them. It was a great privilege for me to meet my relatives and also introduce them to my growing family. My mom got to visit her birthplace and the place where my great-grandparents are buried.

The stadium in Osaka was huge and boasted a new track with a fast surface, thanks to new technology. The weather was humid and hot. The meet started fine for me. I ran 10.44 in the 100, close to my decathlon personal best. Andrei Krauchanka false-started twice, blatantly, and was disqualified, leaving the field that much more open. Roman did poorly in the 100 and looked a little sluggish. Jamaica's Maurice Smith ran a personal best of 10.62 in heat two, a clear statement that he was there to win.

> If I finished a meet, I usually won it . . . but I was not dominating as I had before.

I had the longest long jump of the competition, 7.65 (25 feet 1 inch), and looked on my way to a great meet. I hopped out of the sand pit and punched my fist in the air, knowing that somewhere in the stands, behind the pin cushion of flashes, my family was watching me.

But Maurice Smith came within 9 centimeters (3.5 inches) of his personal best in the shot put, launching into first place in spite of my 15.51-meter (50 feet 10.5 inches) throw. Tom Pappas had jumped into third place, and Roman was in fourth, ready to make a play for the lead.

In the high jump I expected to regain the lead over Maurice. I took my first jump and soared over the bar with room to spare. I lined up for the second attempt at 2.00 meters (6 feet 6.7 inches) and was relaxed and feeling great. I ran toward the bar, but on the last step, my foot slipped, my leg buckled, and I fell into the pit.

People sometimes wonder how you can injure yourself doing something as simple as jumping. They do not realize that decathletes are constantly performing at the body's peak capabilities. There are no easy events. Hurling your body six feet in the air is not normal behavior. We are running and jumping and throwing close to human limits. Getting off just a bit can cause disaster. Just like a race car whose body and engine are precisely designed and calibrated—with different PSIs for the inside and outside tires, and everything measured to the ounce—a decathlete's body is sculpted and trained to compete in specific ways. Like a nudge that can send a race car into the wall at 200 miles per hour, so a seemingly small misstep can take a decathlete down.

That's what happened to me in Osaka.

I limped away from the pit, my leg already whining with pain. Instead of trying again at that height, I decided to rest and try later at 2.03. But my leg did not go along with the plan. The more I rested, the more my leg tightened up. I lined up and took a run at the bar but failed to make 2.03 on three jumps, my leg complaining the whole time. I was now the proud owner of third place. My coaches and I headed under the stadium to meet with the team doctor.

> We are running and jumping and throwing close to human limits. Getting off just a bit can cause disaster.

"It's all knotted up," he said, referring to the muscle he was palpating in my leg. "Strained quad. Nothing I can do."

Giving up was never good enough for my coaches or me, so I tried acupuncture and jogging, but the leg would not loosen up. There was no way I could run a 400. The high jump would be my last event. Roman ended up with gold, Maurice with silver (making Jamaica a very happy place that night), and Dmitri Karpov with bronze.

I ended up with bitter disappointment.

My family, coaches, and I had come all that way, with high expectations, only to watch me miss one step and injure myself. My coaches and I started to question what we were doing wrong. Were we not building in enough recovery time? What was my body telling me?

We concluded, perhaps a little tardily, that I had not taken enough downtime. After Osaka I went to Seattle and stayed away from the track the rest of the summer. The break could not have been more welcome. My coaches and I just wanted 2007 to end so we could start fresh.

Each competition was bringing me closer to 2008 and Beijing. Before getting there, however, I would face a whole new set of challenges that would take me to my mental and physical limits.

THIRTEEN
UNBELIEVABLE PRESSURE

After avoiding the track for a couple of months, I felt my health return, and I began to look forward to competing again. I got back into the weight room, onto the track, and in the daily rhythm of training. Memories of 2007 faded into the background.

By early 2008, the intensity of the Olympics was fully upon me. People had been asking all along, "Do you think you will win the gold in 2008?" My answer always was the same: "That's the plan." But so many things can go wrong that I knew there was no certainty, not even on the last lap of the last event. I had successfully kept away from Olympics speculation by concentrating on each meet, each event, each practice, and especially my family life.

I won the 2008 World Indoor Championships, posting a personal best 6,371 points. It was fitting that the heptathlon helped me get back in sync. I have always enjoyed the hep, maybe because with only seven events and no 1500, it is a lot easier than having to do a dec. I enjoy being indoors; the crowd tends to feel bigger and louder. It is a controlled environment, so you do not have to worry about the weather. Yet it can also be a bit strange: you are indoors from dawn to dark, and you never see the sun.

When the 2008 Olympics arrived, the weight of expectations proved almost unbearable. Everything important to me—my marriage, family, income, professional goals, and dreams—would be changed by this one performance. It wasn't like football or basketball, where you can rely on your teammates to bail you out. The winning Super Bowl team gets 150 rings to distribute among its players, coaches, and staff. Even the injured guys and the practice squad get rings. But in the decathlon only one person receives an Olympic gold medal. Only one person stands on that highest podium and listens to his national anthem. Nobody is there to pick up the slack if you are having a bad day, get sick or injured, or botch an event.

It was all on me.

I could not help thinking about it. If I did not win the gold medal, my wife would have to return to work just to help us pay the bills. We had bought a small house, and Sarah was living her dream of staying home full-time with Jacob and Kate. I was supporting us through sponsorships. I was blessed. My contract with Nike allowed me to train full-time. I had earned a bonus by winning silver in 2004. There is not a lot of money in the decathlon, but as one of the top decathletes in the world, I was making a living at it. The pressure was constantly on me

> "Do you think you will win the gold in 2008?" My answer always was the same: "That's the plan."

to perform well. My contract stipulated that I had to maintain a top-three world ranking every year, or they would cut my base salary. If I finished out of the medals in Beijing, my sponsorships would effectively end. I would not be able to pay my bills, and I would have to get a "real" job. All the fame and accolades would recede into the past.

Those were the hard facts. I was terrified to think that one small error in any one of the ten events could radically change my life, my wife's happiness, and the trajectory of my professional career. It would even affect what my kids thought of me. Would their dad be an Olympic gold medalist and pro athlete, or a physical education coach at a local high school or college who had won a silver medal way back when?

A loss would also rattle my family relationships. Some members of my extended family still believed I had made a big mistake by marrying at the height of my athletic career. If I failed to win gold, they thought it would be because I was distracted by my wife. This was ridiculous; I had won silver in Athens the year I had gotten married. Having a loving wife and healthy marriage gave me the stability and solid foundation to go out and compete with confidence. Without Sarah, I never would have made the Olympics at all. But some people in my own family couldn't see it that way. If I performed poorly, they would always think my wife had kept me from fulfilling my potential as an athlete.

On an even more personal level, I felt the pressure to perform. What if I did my best, and it wasn't good enough? Could I handle that? What if some other guy came out of nowhere and had the meet of his life, and I never got another shot at the Olympics? What would that say about my talents? Had I overestimated them?

The pressure and expectations also tested my faith. I had believed my calling was to be a track athlete. I had dreams of creating a foundation to help and encourage young people, especially the fatherless ones. I had believed that God was telling me to do these things. If I failed in Beijing, how would I fulfill them? And if

I failed, what would it mean for my calling? Had I wasted the last twenty years of my life? An athlete who is not a Christian has his personal passion and worth on the line, but his performance says nothing about God. I was dealing with serious questions. Is God real? Was I not actually hearing from God? Was I in His will? If I didn't win, had I really been listening to Satan all along? Had I been confused?

Other, smaller concerns weighed me down too. If I lost, I would disappoint not only myself, my coaches, my wife, and my family, but also the state of Hawaii, the United States, which I was representing, and the many American decathlon fans. I would humiliate myself in front of a billion people.

> I was terrified to think that one small error in any one of the ten events could radically change my life, my wife's happiness, and the trajectory of my professional career.

As the pressure built, the urge to quit returned and grew stronger. If I quit, I knew what to expect. I could manage the disappointment. But if I competed, who knew what might happen? I could fail miserably. I thought it would be better to control a known bad outcome rather than submit myself to the uncertainty of competition. The logic doesn't sound convincing to me now, but at the time it made sense. I spent a lot of time and energy fighting mental battles that nobody except Sarah knew about.

One day the stress from all those thoughts became so great that I unburdened myself to my pastor.

"I wish God would just come down, sit in front of me, and tell me, 'Bryan, don't worry. It's all going to happen the way it's supposed to,'" I told him. "The pressure is so bad that I'm even questioning whether I heard from God correctly that this is my calling. What if I don't win the gold? Does that mean I missed God's will for my life?"

I don't remember his response because I was stuck in an echo chamber of anxiety. All I could think about were the consequences of failure.

My mom and I spoke frequently, and she reminded me that this was my destiny. Her confidence was encouraging in its own way, but I became irritated with her.

"Mom, can we not talk about the Olympics?" I asked. "Let's talk about anything else. Anything you want but that."

"That's fine," she said. "But remember: God told me you were going to win the gold medal. Don't worry about it anymore. Everything will be fine."

I wish I could have taken her advice. The subject was so stressful for me that at home we did not talk about the Olympics. Home was a Beijing-free zone, a place of escape where I could be somebody else—a father, a husband, a friend. Sarah was very

> I was stuck in an echo chamber of anxiety.

good about not bringing it up. She gave me complete support and no pressure. When I lay in bed at night, stressed out about not being able to provide the life she wanted because it was all hinging on this gold medal, she never worried with me. She was always supportive. Whatever happened would be fine with her. I couldn't have loved her more.

The only way I got through those terrible yet exciting months was by drawing on the lessons I had learned about how to compete in the midst of extreme stress and high expectations. The wisdom and advice gained through years of training became my lifeline. The lessons were not just useful; they were indispensable. It was as if God had been building my life one block at a time.

Trusting God on the Track

There are a thousand and one ways not to make the USA Olympic team, and in Eugene I came close to finding one. The winds were a little funny on day one of the Olympic Trials—unpredictable, gusty. Still, it felt great to be back there, seven years after I had burst onto the national scene. At least it felt great until the long jump.

I ran the 100 in an impressive 10.39. My mind was relaxed and alert. I felt good. Then I got into the long jump and lost my rhythm. Nobody but my coaches and I knew that, for the better part of a year, I'd had some issues with the long jump. I couldn't find my groove in it. In practice I did fine, but in meets the steps and approach felt off. I hadn't turned in a good jump in a competition all year.

Part of the problem was that I did not compete much in 2008. We were focused on the Olympics, focused on training, and we did not want to chance my getting hurt. The downside was that I got a little rusty. I found it harder to find my timing in an actual meet.

> There are a thousand and one ways not to make the USA Olympic team, and in Eugene I came close to finding one.

I took my first jump, but the approach did not feel smooth. I was distracted, thinking too much about my steps instead of planning them out and letting them flow. The jump was short: 7.39 meters (24 feet 3 inches). I went back to take another, and this time I thought even harder as I stared down the lane. I would make my stride a little longer, try to adjust for the awkward feeling I had. I began running even though I still felt off.

I hit the end of the runway pretty short of the line and did not get a lot of energy into the launch: 7.26 meters (23 feet 10 inches). I was frustrated. What was I doing wrong? How should I adjust? I hated not knowing what the problem was.

My third and final jump was a foul, leaving me with a disappointing 7.39 best jump. There was no hiding now; everybody knew I had underperformed in an event. I felt the familiar conflict inside: the desire to panic and overthink and the wisdom to let the event go and move to the next one without anxiety. Bad days happened for everyone, even on the best events. Sometimes there was no explaining it. I did my best to chalk it up to an off day and move on.

When I got into the shot put ring to practice, I felt off there too. My practice throws hit the ground short. It seemed that no matter what I did, I didn't have a great throw in me. When you are dealing with a sixteen-pound ball, the slightest error is magnified. I couldn't keep pushing it in practice though; I had to save some for the event. Then the panic I had suppressed fairly successfully after the long jump began to creep into my heart. What was happening? Was I really having an off day today—of all days?

I took three throws in the shot, and the best one was 15.17 (49 feet 9 inches), well short of the 15.70 I had hoped for. Whatever margin I wanted to put between me and second place was shrinking fast. Worse, the panic now overwhelmed me. The vision I'd had going into the meet and the reality of what I had done so far looked completely different.

I had pictured myself jumping 7.80 (25 feet 7 inches). Instead, I jumped a foot shy of that. I had seen myself throwing 15.70 (51 feet 6 inches) in shot. I threw a foot and a half shy of that. What did this bode for the high jump, where I wanted to jump between 2.06 and 2.09? What about the 400, where I wanted to run 48.00 seconds?

What did it say about the big lead I had hoped to pile up on day one, setting myself up for an even bigger day two?

That vision was gone.

Usually I gave myself a sense of confidence by pulling away early. Now my competitors were breathing down my neck. My weakness would embolden them. I would have to nail the last seven events and burn through the 1500 to hold on to anything. Beijing, it seemed, was slipping out of my grasp.

My thoughts were broken by the call to warm up for the high jump. I settled into a routine as best I could, cleared my mind, rocked back, started forward, leaped, arched, and banged the bar at a low practice level. I did this two more times and realized I might actually no-height, missing my opening bar.

By now I was in a full-blown crisis of confidence, something that rarely happened to me. I walked off the track while the other athletes did their high jumps, and I buried myself under the bleachers. The thoughts I had been fending off for months came upon me with a vengeance.

Why are you even doing this? I asked myself. *Is this goal worth it? You have no peace. You're going crazy with expectations. If you keep fighting, chances are you'll make a fool of yourself and not live up to everyone's expectations, just like you're doing now. Why not just walk away now? Save yourself the trouble, the humiliation, the exhaustion.*

> My competitors were breathing down my neck. . . . Beijing, it seemed, was slipping out of my grasp.

I had not felt so tempted to quit a meet since that early experience in Edmonton. Temptation is strongest when the goal no longer seems worth the effort and when the disappointment of failure seems easier to live with than the ongoing stress of competition.

So I prayed, almost demanding that God help me get a handle on the meet. I took the Bible's advice and threw all my cares on Him—the expectations, my poor performance thus far, the Olympics, my ultimate destiny, and whatever else I could think of.

God, I don't want to go on with this if I'm just going to lose, I said in my heart. *I need to know right now why this is worth it and how I'm going to pull out of this nosedive.*

There was silence. My questions seemed to echo and fade away, signaling epic futility. Disappointed and angry, I walked back to the high jump area, and on my way I heard God answer me: *Bryan, I do not expect you to be perfect. I just expect you to do your best. I'll make it good enough.*

In an instant the strain and stress of expectations drained away. My heart felt lighter, my mind suddenly free. I stopped and considered the words that were impressed deep on my heart. I could not doubt them. They changed everything. I knew now I did not have to win the Olympics. I didn't even have to make the team. All I had to do was to offer my best. God would take care of the results. It was a promise I would cling to because I had nothing else.

> Temptation is strongest when the goal no longer seems worth the effort and when the disappointment of failure seems easier to live with than the ongoing stress of competition.

My turn came in the high jump. I was no longer thinking 2.09 meters or even 2.06. I was just hoping to sail cleanly over any height—anything to keep my meet, my dreams, my destiny alive. I lined up and looked at the bar, set at 1.90 meters (6 feet 3 inches). This time I felt almost jubilant, like someone who has nothing to lose.

I took my first step, bounding on an elliptical path toward the bar. By the time I reached it, I was running almost parallel to it. I launched with my right foot and soared high over the bar with five inches to spare. I landed in the pit, rolled backward, saw the bar still sitting on its supports, and felt a surge of confidence. I clapped once and stepped off the pit. My mojo was back.

I did not stop there. I kept moving the bar up and kept clearing the heights. Finally I was up to 2.08 meters, less than an inch below my personal best. I felt great now. My posture was more upright as I began my approach. My steps fell right where they needed to; I pushed off with the right foot, put my hand over, then my back, and finally my legs in one continuous, flowing arch. I did not come close to the bar. I rolled upright in the pit, saw that I had done it, and pumped two fists in the air. The crowd cheered for me.

I was doing my best, and God was making it good enough. Not only that but I was having the time of my life.

In the 400, I ran 48.41, hitting my goal, and at the end of the day I was somehow in the lead, though only by 22 points, too close for comfort.

Day two was like butter. I killed the hurdles with a personal best time of 13.75 and nailed the discus and the pole vault. I had a monster javelin throw, 20 feet farther than my nearest competitor, and I felt as relaxed as I had in years. Even the 1500 was a not-too-shabby 4:50.97.

All I had to do was to offer my best. God would take care of the results.

After collapsing on the grass and catching my breath, I walked over to the stands to hug Sarah and pick up Jacob, who turned three that day. I carried him with me as I waved to the crowd. I not only made the team, but I won with a personal best score of 8,832 points, an Olympic Trials record and the second-highest score in American history (behind—guess who—Dan O'Brien). Trey Hardee finished second with 8,534 points, and Tom Pappas grabbed the third spot with 8,511, becoming the first American to make three Olympic decathlon teams.

I couldn't believe that a day earlier I had almost thrown the whole thing away.

I liked the headline I saw in the *Los Angeles Times* when I got home a few days later: "Clay Leaves All of His Doubts in the Dust." In the midst of high competition, on the biggest stage in the world, God was still teaching me. I did not have to be perfect. It was a fantasy that I could be. Rather, I had to give my best. It was a principle I had to put into practice every day. I would see how it worked again in the world's most prestigious competition.

My performance at Trials drew the spotlight, and for the next month it shone brightly on me, leading up to Beijing. The freedom from expectations I had experienced in Eugene was, in some ways, short-lived. I knew in my head that I should relax and do my best, but often I could not keep myself from anticipating the games and thinking about the consequences. Media outlets, including major television networks and magazines, were clamoring for interviews and photo shoots and footage of me to use in the run-up. Requests came into Paul Doyle, and he handled them deftly, but the media schedule was distracting and pulled me out of my mental game. Suddenly I was right back in the vortex of worry, but in the back of my mind, I knew the answer was simply to trust God.

Everyone around me knows that I am not the most pleasant person to be with when a meet is coming up. My wife calls it PMS: "premeet syndrome." A couple of weeks out I become so focused, my mind wrapped up in it, that I get irritable about everything else. I do not like to make a lot of decisions during this time. I want things to be calm, quiet, and easy. I feel bad for Sarah and my coaches (and anyone else who comes in contact with me) for having to deal with me.

In a blur of training and photo shoots and a thousand small decisions, I had to pack for China. Sarah and my family would arrive later. As a surprise for me, Sarah had e-mailed all my friends and family and asked them to write letters of encouragement to me. She put everything in a book and gave it to me when I was getting ready to board the plane. During that long, lonely flight, I spent hours reading and rereading the heartfelt letters from my grandparents, mom, dad, stepdad, brother, and many relatives and friends. They reminded me that even though there was unbelievable pressure to perform, if things did not go the way we all hoped, I was coming home to people who loved me. It would not matter to them if I won a medal or not.

My son Jacob's note in particular made me cry. "Daddy, you run really fast and do a good job," he wrote. "You're the best daddy in the whole world. I love you. Hebrews 13:6: 'So we can say with confidence, the Lord is my helper, so I will have no fear.'"

That was one of the verses Jacob had memorized to help him not be afraid at night. To know that my son was drawing strength from the Bible just as I was touched me deeply and pulled me back to center. Track was fun and important, but being a father to my son and daughter was more important by a mile. That book and those letters remained a comfort to me during my entire experience in China, and many times I slipped away to look over the book and consider how blessed I was to have those people in my life.

Preparing for My Biggest Meet

Olympic representatives met the American athletes at the Beijing airport and took us by bus through the city. The freeway was completely clear of vehicles, and we had a police escort. I had been to Beijing once before, in 2001 for the World University Games, but this time it looked completely different. The air was clear, and the streets were clean. I didn't even recognize the place.

I arrived at Olympic Village and met the USA coaching staff. They gave room assignments and keys to all the athletes; told us when our team meetings were; where the doctor, massage therapist, and cafeteria were; the hours of breakfast and track practice; and so on. I also got a bagful of competition gear. I was jet-lagged but had to stay awake until bedtime, so I found a warm-up track and went for a jog. After calling my family, I hit the hay early, staying in the Village that first night.

When my coaches arrived the next day, we moved to a nearby condo we had rented. Some athletes get hyped up and social during the Olympics; others, like me, want to be alone. I like to feel in control of my environment the closer I get to a meet. I don't want a lot of noise. I want to be surrounded by people I know. I don't even want the wrong music. I'm in a holding pattern until the meet starts, and I can relax.

Olympic Village or any location close to the stadium is anything but relaxing. Countless distractions surround the games, and if you pay attention to the sideshow, you can fritter away your energy. Decathletes have it even harder because we compete toward the end when other athletes have moved on to partying and celebrating. I had to stay away from the noise and conserve my energy for competition.

The field of competition in the decathlon was almost exactly the same in 2008 as in 2004. Most of the guys I saw in Athens were there. The Czech Republic again sent Tomas and Roman. Russia sent some decent decathletes, as did Germany and some smaller countries from Europe and Asia.

I had so much experience that I felt like one of the "old" guys even though I was still in my twenties. That's what happens when you start making national teams when you are still in college. I was in my eighth year of competition, and I felt as if I had been around forever. Watching some of the less experienced guys warm up, I realized I had an advantage. Experience had taught me how to handle the rough patches. I might do poorly in one event, but I might do really well in another. The decathlon offered many chances to come back.

I had to just do what I do and stick to the principles I had learned through training and in my walk with God.

After the colossal, spectacular opening ceremony in Beijing, the 116 members of the USA track and field team flew to a coastal resort where we would train and relax until it was our turn. The resort offered a lot of opportunities for diversion: a golf simulator, a bowling alley, and many places to hike on the huge property. The place was empty of other guests and secure all the way around so we had no contact with anyone but American Olympians and coaches. Honestly, it felt a little eerie.

We were also under a media "block-out." The television in the cafeteria, around which we gathered to watch the Olympics, showed only the Chinese teams. We got glimpses of how other countries did in highlight packages. The Internet was limited, and certain pages apparently were blocked by the government. I had the unsettling feeling of being watched and directed all the time.

The one thing we did pick up from the coverage was that the USA track and field team was having a very uneven Olympics. A few athletes were having the best meets of their lives, but the majority were having the worst meets of their lives. Favored athletes were making glaring mistakes. These were people I knew, people who had been at the resort with me until just days earlier. They had disappeared from the resort and shown up on the television screen only to look diminished and uncertain. I had seen them compete for years; I knew some of their marks and knew they were supposed to win these events. To see them do poorly was perplexing. What was going on? Was it something in the water?

Day after day, groups of athletes left the resort for Beijing to compete. Day after day, the results looked the same: either really good or, in most cases, really bad. Eventually the only people left were the decathletes

> Experience had taught me how to handle the rough patches. I might do poorly in one event, but I might do really well in another.

and marathoners—the only athletes who compete after us. There was a certain irony in the fact that as Olympic athletes we had watched most of the games on limited Chinese broadcasts from a city hundreds of miles away.

Watching on the last day at the resort with my coaches, I couldn't help saying, "Man, what is going on? The way this has gone so far it will be either my best decathlon or my worst. I don't see any in-between happening. I'll be the standout story for track and field, or I'll get thrown in with the rest of those who didn't show up."

My coaches did not know how to respond, except to be encouraging as they always were. In a way, the poor results focused my mind even more. I determined that no matter what anyone else was doing, I was going to do my best to have a good meet. It also took off the pressure to think that I would do really well or really badly. Having two possible outcomes instead of a thousand seemed to take the unpredictability out of the whole thing.

The next morning I packed my bags, said good-bye to the resort, and left for Beijing—and the meet of my life.

FOURTEEN
A TIME TO WIN IT ALL

I woke up at 5:00 a.m. on the day of my Olympic competition, grabbed my iPod, and went down to the street to do my premeet warm-up as I always do. My routine welcomed me. I felt surprisingly relaxed and focused, given the enormous expectations for my performance. The sky was dark; the sounds of Beijing city life were stirring. I started some easy drills and light jogging to get the blood moving before my real warm-up. People passing by probably had no idea that in a matter of hours they could watch me live from the Beijing National Stadium as I embarked on the most important two-day span of my career.

Jogging back to the hotel for breakfast, I felt something hit me. A raindrop. It was starting to drizzle.

Classic decathlon weather, I thought sardonically. *They never make it easy.* For the past three weeks we had enjoyed almost constant sunshine at the coastal resort. Now the dawn revealed a thick gray sky. *At least it's not hot*, I thought optimistically as the rain pelted me harder. *Maybe the clouds will burn off as they do in California. It might be a nice day.*

The weather was just one more complication to deal with in the run-up to the climactic event of my life.

Back at the hotel I ate my breakfast—oatmeal—and listened to a mix of worship music and country music on my headphones. I had entered my zone. My coaches gestured now and then to inquire if I needed anything, but we kept communication to a minimum. They knew it was my time to be alone, to get centered, to prepare my mind for what was ahead. Those hours leading up to the event had always proved critical to success.

Riding in a taxi to the warm-up track, I eyed the weather. Instead of burning off, the clouds were getting darker and the rain heavier. I only smiled. Now that it was obviously going to be a rainy meet, I welcomed it. It took my mind back to Hawaii where it rained on our track meets all the time. The rain might even give me an advantage against other athletes. I recalled the 2005 World Championships in Helsinki—raining, 50 degrees, the wind blowing seemingly out of the Arctic. And I went out and had one of the best meets of my life.

If anybody can compete in the rain, it's me, I thought as we entered the stadium, commonly known as the "Bird's Nest," cameras and video cameras following my every step. It was an unusually upbeat assessment from me, but I had learned to be confident about my chances since Athens and Helsinki. I was becoming more like my mom: certain that at some point I would do what used to seem impossible.

On the track I walked through each event slowly and methodically. I thought about each step in the 100. I went through the long jump, counting my steps and picturing what it would feel like to fly through the air. I pictured gliding and hurling the shot. More than ever I felt like my grandfather, Jiji, relentlessly seeking perfection in every detail of my work. The same drive for excellence that helped him build a successful food business had helped to bring me this far. Now it was time to finish the job.

After walking through and visualizing each event, I came back to the covered tent in the infield where athletes were relaxing and getting massages. The skies were pouring rain, and I heard some of them complaining.

"Perfect weather. Just perfect."

"Why does it always wait to rain until the decathlon?"

Some of them paced around, looking tight and upset. The weather was messing with their mental games. But not mine. The rainier it got, the better I felt. I spotted Roman. We had battled hard on the track the past four years, but we enjoyed each other's company as much as ever. Grinning, we shook hands and started taking pictures of each other, goofing off in the rain.

"This is the hardest I've ever seen it rain, even in Hawaii," I said, struggling to be heard over the downpour.

He shrugged, just as unperturbed as I was. "Oh, well," he said in his heavy Czech accent. "What are you going to do?"

His response was a reminder of why I liked Roman. Nothing touched the guy. And this morning nothing was touching me. It was shaping up to be a good day.

The stadium soon filled up, in spite of the rain, and the first event got under way—the 100. I put my starting blocks in place, knelt into my stance, and waited for the gun. Every second seemed like an hour. *Bang!* Before I knew what I was doing, I was flying down the track, my body performing the task with hardly a need for conscious thought. Every step fell where it should. I felt loose and relaxed, moving faster than most people dream of running.

Ten seconds later I blasted across the finish line just shy of a personal best. Around me I heard the curses and angry expressions from the other runners. The wet rubber track had spooked them, and they all fell well short of their normal times. Advantage: Clay.

I rolled through the long jump and the shot put with what felt like ease. My shot put throw was a personal best of 16.27 meters (53 feet 4.5 inches), not bad for the biggest event I had ever competed in. I saw my coaches smiling, and I couldn't help smiling too. Though I made a habit of never looking at my score during a meet, I knew I must be putting a lot of points between the other guys and me. Many of them were clearly frustrated. Some walked around talking vehemently to themselves; others fumed and paced. Others consulted with their coaches. But I was flying high. The pressure of the previous four years faded into the background. I was where I belonged, on the track, where I controlled my destiny.

Then out of nowhere, the high jump assaulted me.

A Near Disaster

I have always liked the high jump. I am good at it, and I feel confident at it. And that day was no different. I cleared the first two heights easily and had the bar moved up to 1.99 meters (6 feet 6 inches). I fully intended to go higher than that, but I had to get there safely and incrementally, moving my score up by a few centimeters at a time. I lined up for my first jump at the new height, readied myself, and ran toward the bar. Nothing seemed to bother me, not the wet ground, not the attitudes of the other athletes, not the pressure of a billion sets of eyeballs watching me on televisions around the globe.

And just like that, I missed my first jump. *A fluke*, I thought, getting up from the pit. *No biggie.* You get three attempts to clear each height. I lined up again, ready to soar over the bar.

I ran, leaped, and knocked the bar again, missing my second

jump. Now I felt a little hitch inside. My sense of control was slipping as I walked back to the starting line.

"Come on, Bryan," I heard one of my coaches say from behind me in the stands, where coaches were required to stay. "Let's do this."

I readied myself for the third jump, took an extra moment at the line to picture my steps and a successful launch, and then took off, hurling myself over the bar. Too early; it grazed my shoulder and fell down with me onto the bag. In a matter of seconds I had blown the high jump. My stellar meet came crashing to earth.

Stunned, I put my hands on my head and walked away.

You just gave away the gold medal, I told myself, heart pounding in double time. *You had it, but you let it go.*

Without even going to the stands to talk with my coaches I walked off the track toward the holding room and felt my emotions spiraling downward with each step.

Failure, I thought. *This is it. This is what it feels like. You just wasted your life. All that buildup just to humiliate yourself in front of the entire world. Some Olympic favorite.*

Bewildered, I disappeared under the stadium and made my way through the cold concrete corridors. I felt as if I had been mugged. Then like seeing a light flickering in a dark tunnel, I remembered Eugene. I had been in this situation before—same failure, same emotions, same response. For a moment the cascade of negative feelings stopped, and my personal sun broke through the clouds.

Remember what you learned in Eugene, I heard in my heart.

I ducked into the locker room and found a private place to think and pray, away from the constant movement of the competition and the noise and flashes of cameras in the stands.

I remembered what had saved me at the Olympic Trials.

"God doesn't expect me to be perfect," I repeated to myself. "He expects me to give my best, and He'll make it good enough."

It was a nice thought, and maybe it worked in a small town in Oregon with nobody watching, but what about in China on the biggest Olympic stage in history? Would that spiritual principle work against the world's greatest athletes? Or was I fooling myself? Was this just one of those good luck charms or superstitions that athletes use to pump up their confidence?

I flashed back to the meet in Eugene. I had felt mentally, physically, and emotionally incapable of finishing on my own. I had cried out to God and asked for an answer, an intervention—anything. And He had answered, and I had won by a wide margin.

If it had worked then . . .

I was not going to turn my back on Him now.

> "God doesn't expect me to be perfect," I repeated to myself. "He expects me to give my best, and He'll make it good enough."

"God," I prayed, "You know I just had a terrible high jump. I even may have put myself out of the medal race. But with You all things are possible. I need Your help to fulfill my dream of getting this gold medal. On my own I don't have what it takes. All the physical preparation in the world is not enough. I need the strength, confidence, peace, and power that only You can provide. Hear me, Lord, and answer me in my time of need."

I listened for His reply. The silence under the stadium was calming. A few athletes passed in and out, marking time between competitions. Bags unzipped; people sighed and groaned. Showers turned on and off. I could hear my heart beating.

Then came the familiar answer: *Go out and do your best, and I will take care of the rest.* The confidence that had engulfed me in Eugene came over me again. I knew what I needed to do.

"Okay, Lord," I said in reply. "You've got a deal. I'm going to go out and do my best. You're going to have to make it good enough."

Moments later I settled into the blocks for the 400. While other runners were busy visualizing their race or pumping themselves up, I was repeating: "Lord, I'm going to give it my best effort, but You'll have to make it good enough."

Bang! The gun went off. We surged forward, came around the first curve and down the straightaway. I was in the middle of the pack but was hanging in there. Because of the rain, the speed of the race was slower than normal. As we rounded the last curve, the 400-meter specialists turned on the afterburners and pulled away. I crossed the line with a respectable but not great time. It was nowhere near a personal best. But I did not panic or get emotional. I held on to what God had said to me, and then I reminded Him of His promise. "Lord, I did my best," I told Him as I cooled down. "Now it's time for You to live up to Your end of the deal."

I stepped into the infield to watch subsequent heats. The first one went as slowly as ours, as if someone had turned down the master control on everyone's speed. It happened again in the third heat and the fourth and the fifth. Everyone was looking tentative. I could hardly believe my eyes. When the event was done, my time compared favorably to the rest of the field. I had not fallen behind.

"Thank You, God," I said, amazed at what had just unfolded.

I went back to my hotel with a greater peace than I had ever experienced during a competition. Usually my mind races with thoughts of the next day as if I could win the events by envisioning them a

> "God . . . I even may have put myself out of the medal race. But with You all things are possible."

thousand times. But this time I knew everything would work out. I had done my job, put in the work, and given it my best effort. I would do the same tomorrow, and God would take care of the final result.

Finishing the Job

The next day was hot, nearly 100 degrees on the track, the opposite of the day before. Athletes were already dropping out of the competition. That morning I went through the first three events like butter, smoothly executing the 110-meter hurdles, the discus, and the pole vault.

Then came the ninth event, the javelin. For all its difficulty, the javelin had become one of my favorite events for a number of reasons. It takes place late enough in the meet that the crowds are usually bigger. People are paying attention to the action in the decathlon and the other events that are wrapping up. The javelin runway also backs up into the lanes of the track, putting the athletes close to the fans and creating a personal connection. Fans love to see the javelin fly, so they clap and cheer more than at other events.

From a competitive viewpoint I also consider it the decisive event in any meet. If I am in the lead, the javelin is where I want to deliver the finishing blow to my opponents, especially since the final event, the 1500 meters, is one of my weaker events. If I am behind going into the javelin, it offers one last chance to fight for the lead. No matter how tired I am, I always try to find a little bit of extra juice to put into my jav throw. It is the defining moment.

But this time was different.

Only my coaches and I knew that my throwing arm was killing me. I had torn the labrum, a ring of cartilage in my shoulder, a few years ago and had been putting up with the pain ever since. To make it worse, my elbow was hurting badly from missing my form a few times. Though I loved the javelin, it had become one of my toughest events. Now I was doing it with an injury in the Olympic Games.

Once again, the decathlon had probed and found my weakest spot.

I hoisted the javelin and felt a twinge in my injured shoulder. Ahead of me were 118 feet of rubberized track—the runway where I would build up speed and launch the javelin as far as humanly possible. I looked over at my coaches, leaning over the railing in the stands. They nodded. Good to go. I gripped the jav two-thirds of the way back on the shaft and held it—all 8.5 feet of it—just above my shoulder. I began to run.

As usual I had preplanned the number of strides and the length of each one. I began taking the stutter steps toward the mark, then the loping crossover steps toward the line. Three steps, four steps, five steps, hold, then a quick six-seven to set me up—and I came to a sudden stop, my whole body pivoting to release the built-up energy through my arm, hurling the javelin up and out like a stone out of a slingshot. It arced, leveled, and descended, spearing the ground. Judges ran up to measure the distance. Thousands of people cheered, but I didn't hear them. I was thinking about my shoulder and elbow, both in serious

> Only my coaches and I knew that my throwing arm was killing me. . . . Though I loved the javelin, it had become one of my toughest events.

pain. I must have reinjured them. I knew they were in no shape to be competing at an Olympic level. My arm tingled and throbbed, and I could barely keep from grimacing.

I walked back to the start line and waited for my coaches' judgment. It hadn't been a great throw, so I wasn't completely surprised when Coach Barnett yelled, "Can you take another one?" while eyeing my shoulder. He could tell it was bothering me more than usual. I straightened up my posture to mask any sign of pain.

As I walked back to the start line, my right shoulder was having a screaming match with my brain. It was in full revolt against what I was putting it through. The javelin had preyed on me for the past couple of years. Something about the amount of force being channeled through the arm, all that stress whipping through the joints, bones, muscles, and ligaments messed me up physically more than other events did. I was being reminded with vivid pain how the decathlon picks your body apart.

I grabbed a javelin, put those thoughts aside, and strode toward the starting line as if in perfect condition. But even the simple motion of carrying something hurt.

"God, I promised You that I would do my best, and I'm going to hold up my end of the commitment," I said under my breath.

I stood at the back of the runway, my fingers numb. I knew this next throw would hurt. It might even destroy my arm for good. If that happened, this would be the last throw of my career. I had a choice: I could go the safe route and stay within my limits. Or I could go for gold.

I made up my mind. I spoke to myself with authority: *I'm going to throw this thing as hard as I possibly can. If it means I blow out my elbow or my shoulder, so be it. If it means I retire and never compete again, so be it. This is my time. I'm going for the gold medal.*

With that surge of confidence, I turned around to face the crowd. They were already fixed on me as I prepared for my second throw. With the javelin in one hand I began to make exaggerated clapping motions over my head, as I had seen Tomas do way back in Edmonton. Soon the entire stadium was clapping in unison with me. Flashes popped everywhere. I gave out a war whoop and then turned around to face the runway.

The rhythmic clapping of the stadium began to consume me. The beats were at a walking pace. But once I started running, they would speed up, matching each of my steps, and then the crowd would explode as I launched the missile.

I rocked back on one foot and heard the mesmerizing drumbeat one last time. As soon as I started running, it all disappeared—the sounds, the sights, the feeling of the crowd. I had reached the zone, the place that every athlete strives for. I felt as if I was in the stadium alone.

I burst off the line, the javelin poised behind my right ear, gaining speed with great, high strides. *Bam-bam-bam-bam.* I pounded down the track, hitting my marks and summoning every ounce of energy from my heels to the tips of my fingers to unleash into this projectile. I pulled up at the line and with a massive yell flung the shaft up into the air. It grew smaller as it flew away. For a moment it was just me and the javelin, soaring in the night sky, no noise, not even a hush. When you throw it well, the javelin almost disappears. You only see the tail of it until it noses down and knifes into the grass.

> I had a choice: I could go the safe route and stay within my limits. Or I could go for gold.

This time the pain in my arm kept me from seeing where it landed. But I knew from the throw that it had flown farther than before.

The sights and sounds of the crowd came rushing back. The stadium was rocking with delight. But my shoulder shrieked with red, flaring pain that flashed through the whole right side of my body. I didn't even look at the board to see how far the javelin had gone. I was only interested in my coaches' expressions. Was it enough? Or did I have to go again?

I no longer felt my arm. It was inert, dangling against my right side. I couldn't throw a Wiffle ball, let alone a spear, even if Olympic gold depended on it. I just may have ruined my career after all.

But I couldn't think those thoughts now. I might need a third throw. I had to block the pain. In defiance of it I lifted my hands in victory, and the crowd cheered so loudly that my ears rang. I walked back to the start line and looked over at my coaches: Was it good enough, or did I have to take another attempt? They watched the result board carefully. Then they nodded.

"That's good, Bryan," Coach Barnett said, as relieved as I was. "You don't need to take another throw."

I walked over to them, cradling my arm.

"That was awesome," Rana said.

"Even if I needed to take another throw, I don't think I could," I said quietly. "It hurts that bad."

"Take a rest," Coach Barnett said. "You've earned it."

> The sights and sounds of the crowd came rushing back. The stadium was rocking with delight.

I felt a familiar surge of satisfaction at completing nine of the ten events—the javelin had once again proved a high point. The crowd was with me. The heat had broken, and it was starting to cool off just in time for the 1500. I stayed by my coaches, and we chatted a bit, keeping the mood light even as I babied my arm. I knew I had a lead, but in the decathlon no lead is safe. Now I became desperately curious to know where I stood in the competition.

"Where am I at in the totals?" I asked. "Is anybody close? What do I need to do in the fifteen?"

"Don't worry about it," Coach Barnett said dismissively. "Just get ready for it."

"Yeah, but how close are the other guys?" I said. "What kind of time do I have to get? Are we in the clear yet?"

"Just focus on the last event," Rana said.

I kept bugging them. Finally, Kevin, Rana, and Coach Barnett looked at me squarely, if reluctantly, and said, "All you have to do is finish, and you've won. You don't have to run anything special. Just finish the fifteen."

The words sank in, and I realized I was one race away from winning Olympic gold. Could it really be? Was I that close to accomplishing my dream, the destiny my mother had been telling me about for so many years? Dreams had been false advertisements for me in so many ways, all promise and no delivery. Would this one become real? I felt like laughing and crying, and I almost did both at once.

Later I found out that I had the largest lead going into the tenth event in Olympic history. I was ahead by more than 400 points, a huge number. But by this time the rest of the field and I were running on pure adrenaline, which is all we had left after expending ourselves for nine events. And upon hearing that I was close to capturing gold, the adrenaline suddenly drained out of me. The competitive tension I had stored and managed for two days disappeared. I lost every ounce of energy.

I knew I had a lead, but in the decathlon no lead is safe.

Anyone who tells you that the decathlon is not an endurance event doesn't know what he is talking about. It is as much an endurance event as a marathon. You have to stay focused every minute of the two days and ten events. You have to keep your energy high enough to perform well but not so high you burn out quickly. It is a mental game the whole way through.

And now my coaches had done the worst thing possible for me. They had allowed my pestering them to force them into telling me that I had pretty much won. With that, my mental game was blown.

A Final Challenge

Feeling a sense of premature relief and overwhelming fatigue, I walked away from the stands and sat on the infield near a bench. Moments before, I had felt as emotionally high as at any point in my life, knowing that the gold medal was within reach. Now my emotions plunged the other way. I was supposed to be resting and preparing for the final event, but I could barely think of getting off the ground. I had given everything in the nine previous events, and I was crashing—hard.

As the cameras trained on me to feed the sight of an Olympian on the cusp of victory, viewers around the globe surely thought I was savoring this moment at the pinnacle of athleticism. In reality I was panicking. I didn't have the energy even to walk out of the stadium to catch a taxi to my hotel, let alone run around the track nearly four times with some of the fastest people in the world.

> I had given everything in the nine previous events, and I was crashing—hard.

I opened my eyes. The Bird's Nest crowd swam before me like a heat mirage. The scene was surreal. And I was in a panic. I glimpsed Roman sitting not far away. He had competed poorly during the games and was out of the medal hunt. Roman and I are alike in many ways, both extreme competitors as well as devoted family men. I thought back to the time we had spent together with our families in Prague after the Athens Olympics. His son was two or three at the time, and when he saw me, he asked Roman what I was doing there. He knew that his dad and I competed against each other—and now the enemy was in his house. Roman explained that yes, we competed, but we were also friends. We all had a good laugh over it.

That is typical of relationships between decathletes. We are a platoon. Unlike other sports that are highly individualized, the decathlon breeds a special camaraderie and sense of shared mission among competitors. We bond because of the stress and training we all go through to compete. Only a decathlete knows what it takes to do those ten events. Just finishing a meet is an accomplishment. In no other sport do all the finishers take a victory lap together.

True to that spirit, Roman and I had helped each other during previous competitions. One time at the World Indoor Championships in Budapest, something wasn't feeling right about my high jump. My coaches weren't there, so I went to Roman and said, "Dude, what's going on with me?" Roman coached me during the high jump: "You're jumping from too far away. Do this instead." On another occasion I saw Roman having a hard time in the shot put. He walked over to me and threw his hands up in exasperation. I said, "Roman, you're landing open. Do this and this instead."

That kind of thing only happens in the decathlon. You will never see a 100-meter runner or swimmer turn to the guy next to him and say, "Do this to improve your time."

Now Roman came over to me.

"Well, Bryan, it looks like you did it. Congratulations."

Nobody was paying much attention to us because the javelin event was still taking place.

"What do you mean, congratulations? I'm a wreck," I told him. "I can't finish. I'm completely spent. There's nothing left in me."

He smirked coolly. "Bryan, you'll be fine," he said. "Trust me. I know how you feel."

I realized that was true. He knew what I was feeling because he had been through it in 2004. But back then I had been the one battling him for the gold. He, too, had gone into the 1500 knowing that it was his to lose, and that if he blew it, I was right on his heels to claim it.

"Yes, but I have no energy," I said.

"You will do it," he said lazily. "Me, I'm not going to run the fifteen. But you are going to finish."

Now it was my turn to admonish him.

"You've got to run," I protested. "You can't end your career this way. You're the reigning gold medalist. I ran when you won the 2004 Olympics. I was there for you when you won. It won't be right if you don't finish. You've got to do the victory lap."

"I don't want to run," he said. "You can do it on your own. I know you can."

"No, Roman," I almost begged, "you don't understand. I have nothing left. I don't think I can finish this. Please pace me. Otherwise, I won't get through the event."

"You don't understand. I have nothing left. I don't think I can finish this."

I could tell that he, too, was completely taxed and just wanted to be done. His performance was disappointing to him. He had his gold medal and the world record. He had nothing more to prove.

I pressed further: "You're the world record holder and the reigning Olympic champion. You have to run. It won't be the same if you're not there when I cross the finish line."

He looked at me with a sense of brotherly obligation.

"All right," he said with a sigh. "I'll run. But I'm not running fast."

Relief washed over me, and I felt a stab of hope. I retreated to my bench to wait. I still did not know whether I could pull it off, but with Roman's help I could at least try.

Moments later I lined up for the 1500 with Roman at my side. I could tell he didn't want to be there. The gun went off, and we began to run. It was obvious that he knew the pace I was most comfortable with. He probably knew my times as well as I did. He stayed with me through the first two laps, guiding me like a lead blocker clearing the way for a running back. All I remember is staring at his back and willing myself to take each individual step. I was hardly feeling my body. On the third lap Roman accelerated, and I tried to keep up to stay in sight of him, but he got too far in front. That's when the mental struggle intensified.

Just finish. Don't mess it up, I kept telling myself when he was gone. But I was getting wobbly. With every step I thought I would lose my balance and fall over. *Just finish, Bryan. Get there. Do your best,* I told myself, remembering my deal with God.

The finish line came swimming into view. Many of the guys had already crossed it and were walking around with hands on their hips. The line seemed to hover in a timeless space for a moment, untouchable, unreal, the culmination of so many dreams, so many promises, so much planning and sacrifice by my wife, my family, my coaches, and me. As I stumbled toward it, hoping not to collapse onto the track, it seemed as if it would recede forever in front of me, always unattainable.

My halting steps ate away at the distance, and casting aside remaining doubts, I lunged across the finish line, veered onto the grass, and fell onto my back. You would have thought I had just completed a marathon. In a way, I had. I heard the crowd roar.

Oh, thank God it's over, I thought. There was no sense of victory or glory—just pure relief. I lay there with absolutely nothing left inside me. But I had done it.

Thank You that it's over, I prayed, looking up into the night sky. The weight of the past eight years lifted off my shoulders like a hot air balloon rising from the ground. I hardly cared about the result, my points, or my place. What mattered was that the pressure was finally gone.

Someone grabbed my hand—Roman.

"Good job," he said. "It's your time." He pulled me to my feet and raised my hand in his as if to say, "World, here is your new champion."

> I hardly cared about the result, my points, or my place. What mattered was that the pressure was finally gone.

The crowd of nearly a hundred thousand went crazy. Other competitors came over and shook my hand, patted me on the back, and congratulated me. I did the same to them. Then we embarked on the most precious tradition in the decathlon—the group victory lap. With my flag held high I led the finishers as we summoned our energy to trot around the track.

At the bottom of some steps I caught sight of Sarah. She was crying, and when I saw her, I began crying too. I kissed her and said the only thing I could think of: "Thank you so much for being here." Athens had been such a disappointment to me because she had not been there. Now, when it mattered most, she was there to witness it all. My mom, brother, stepdad, grandparents, father-in-law, Mr. Hee, and other family members were right behind her. I embraced them, and in a moment a thousand images of my mom praying for me, believing in me, encouraging me flashed through my mind. I hugged her again and gave her a kiss, and my Olympic experience felt complete.

My coaches came over. Our journey together had demanded

extraordinary sacrifice from them and their families. APU had been the most supportive organization I could have asked for. Our ten years of working together had paid off, and I was as happy for them as I was for myself. We hugged and shook hands.

I had won with a 240-point margin, the largest margin since 1972. My final total: 8,791.

Moments later I was standing on the podium in the Bird's Nest, watching the American flag ascend and hearing "The Star-Spangled Banner" ring through that stadium. Winning other major events had done nothing to prepare me for winning the Olympics. It was a mountaintop experience like no other, full of pride in my country, pride in my family and coaches, even pride in my fellow competitors.

And most of all, profound relief.

After the mandatory drug testing and a late-night press conference, my coaches and I went to dinner at a Japanese restaurant. I pulled the gold medal out of my pocket to pass around the table. Each of my coaches held it, marveled at how heavy it was, and studied its beautiful detail. I felt that we had won it together.

Later that night, as I woke up every couple of hours in pain from the performance and famished for yet another midnight snack, I looked over at my nightstand where the medal was perched.

Nope, it wasn't a dream, I thought, feeling a surge of gratitude at the goodness of God.

He had taken me, a kid who by all human logic should have been sitting in a prison somewhere or doing some menial job in a small

235

Hawaiian town, and had put me on top of that podium in front of the world, with the most coveted prize in the decathlon around my neck.

Better than that, He had given me a great wife and children and the privilege of being a husband and father.

I still do not understand why God singled me out—why He made me a promise that I refused to believe for many years, a promise that seemed so unlikely, a promise to use me for good, even when I saw no good in my life. My mother had seen my destiny early on and reminded me of it many times. Now God had brought it to pass.

He had put people around me to guide me: my wife, my mother, my father, my grandfather, my stepdad, my youth pastor, track coaches, spiritual mentors, and countless friends. He rescued me from my mistakes and taught me how to be a man.

The only word that summed it all up was the word running through my mind that night as I slept off the pain of victory in a hotel in Beijing:

Redemption.

FIFTEEN
NEW
VICTORIES

When the post-Olympics media rush settled down, I went back home to resume normal life, whatever that meant. It was hard for me at times to mentally accept that I had won, especially because I had been telling myself I probably wouldn't. Preparing to compete is one thing; preparing for life after winning is another, and I had not given much thought to that.

I knew that other athletes often found themselves in a deep emotional valley after their highest achievements. I resisted that, but something similar was happening to me. It wasn't so much emotional as practical. I woke up each morning in the fall of 2008 with the same thought: *What now?*

Hard Decisions

After winning Olympic gold, I did not get a lot of time to rest. Officials put me through drug tests and stuck me before the cameras for long media interviews. I then flew back to the U.S., where the next 168 hours were a high-speed train ride to places I never thought I would be.

I sat on Oprah's couch and discussed my win, did the same at Late Night with David Letterman, and spoke at a variety of events for the U.S. Olympic Committee. In every place I held up the medal and shared the story of what God had brought me through and the victory He helped me to achieve. The publicity schedule was almost like an eleventh decathlon event, but this one took place in the glare of studio lights, flashbulbs and magazine shoots, and standing at speaker's podiums.

But the sounds of my home were still the sounds of my home, Sarah's and my routines remained largely the same, and soon the conversations turned away from Beijing. Some days it felt as if nothing had happened at all. I naively expected to feel differently overnight, like when I had gotten my driver's license. I wanted life suddenly to be more glamorous, easier, full of fun, and free of pressure. But everything looked, smelled and tasted the same as before. I often would slip back to my bedroom, open the drawer and look at the gold medal. I surely hadn't dreamed it, but it certainly wasn't having the transformative effect I thought it might.

There were a couple of goals I had been considering. One was to medal three times in the Olympics in decathlon. It has never been done. The decathlete who came closest, England's Daley Thompson, won two medals (1980 and 1984) and came in fourth on his third attempt in 1988. My pessimistic side said that perhaps it had never been done because it could not be done. Did I want to spend the next four years chasing an illusion? Would I just run my body and mind into the ground and harm the rest of my life in the attempt?

The most logical step was to keep training to compete in 2009, but my motivation had ebbed. The decathlon in Beijing had been a twelve-year event for me, not just a two-day event. For most of my adult life I had taken my body and mind to places few people go in terms of exhaustion and exertion. It is a massive commitment to try to be the best in the world. Did I want to do it again? I wasn't sure. When you've never done it, you are so hungry for achievement that nothing else matters. But afterward, when you own that place in Olympic history, you almost wonder how you did it—and if you really want to try again.

I knew that physically, I could handle it. I could work through possible injuries and fatigue. I knew the pathway to gold better than my competitors.

But there were other important questions. Could I hold onto my sponsors that whole time? Sponsors are really only interested in you when you are getting publicity. After the Olympics is over, the decathlon recedes into the distant background of the sporting world. When was the last time you read decathlon results in the newspaper?

Would my sponsors stay true to me during the off years? That question would have a direct effect on my ability to compete.

Even more important, what about my family? Would they be willing to go through another four years of struggle and stress just so we could have a shot at another brief moment of triumph? Would training get in the way of my being a father and husband, which was becoming more important with each passing day?

> I wanted life suddenly to be more glamorous, easier, full of fun, and free of pressure.

Those questions distracted me in 2009 and early 2010, and I didn't perform at the level that I could have. I wasn't even able to compete at USA Championships in 2009 because I hurt my hamstring in practice. I got injured, people observed that I wasn't focused, and they were right. As I ran down the track and hurled the shotput and javelin, I kept asking myself if I was willing to give whatever it took to achieve these new goals. Or was I ready to walk away?

Back-to-Back Titles

I should have recognized earlier that I needed time off to recuperate. Accumulated fatigue in my mind and body was weighing me down. Unfortunately my sponsors did not want to hear that I needed a break. I know that sponsorship is a business relationship, but some of my major sponsors seemed to care only about the short term—this season, the next few meets, the next medal, whatever they could get out of me before I finally collapsed. I was disappointed to realize that my goals of competing well in the 2012 Olympics were not their goals. That friction led to a major change that threatened my training, finances, and career.

My mind was also on my growing family. Our Elizabeth (Ellie to us) was born in 2010. It didn't take long to see that she is athletic, pulling herself up on bars and climbing on everything. My mom and dad say she is just like me: always dancing, jumping, walking, running, climbing, and never sitting still for two seconds. Like our other two children, she has been a complete joy. Jacob is excelling at school, reading well beyond his grade level. Kate, our preschooler, enjoys gymnastics, art, and fashion. I wanted to be with all of them and Sarah as much as I could.

I did compete in Gotzis in 2010, winning in the rain against the best decathletes in the world. I also won the world indoor title, the first and only time a heptathlete has won back-to-back world indoor titles. Still, at the end of the year, my ranking dropped to number three. The new number one was a college student from

Oregon, Ashton Eaton, who had broken the world record in the heptathlon, scoring an amazing 6,499 to win the men's heptathlon at the NCAA Indoor Championships. That bested the 6,476 set by Dan O'Brien in Toronto at the 1993 IAAF World Indoor Championships. Even though I felt I deserved a higher ranking since I had a higher score than Ashton in the decathlon that year, I understood those things come and go, and I was happy for him. My sights were set on 2012.

A Needed Change

With my strength regained and my family happily moving forward, I was eager to come back and compete hard in 2011. My mind was now set on medaling a third time in 2012, and I wanted to beat the decathlon world record of 9,026 set by my good friend Roman. I stayed healthy almost the entire season, but just before USA Championships my knee started to complain, and I did not feel prepared to compete. I tried anyway, never wanting to bow out prematurely, and I fell to the ground in the hurdles, hurting the knee even worse. I still managed to make the world championship team, though, hitting my standard of around 8,200 that season, which no one else had done. I wasn't in peak shape, but I was looking forward to Worlds—and hoping I would heal up in time.

My mind was now set on medaling a third time in 2012.

That's when my livelihood nearly collapsed because of a change with my main sponsor. In a *Today Show* appearance for the U.S. Olympic Committee, I wore the Olympic Committee's sponsoring brand, instead of my sponsoring brand. Even though I had cleared it with my lawyers, my sponsor was upset that I had worn a different brand on national television. The purpose of the appearance was to promote the 2012 Olympics. The issue ended up driving us apart.

I had been unhappy with how little this company had used me in its marketing. It seemed as if the company only wanted me on its team so no other brand could have me. I felt I had been bought, put in a closet, and forgotten.

We agreed to go our separate ways, but when that sponsorship ended, so did my paycheck. Suddenly I needed a job, another sponsor—something to pay the bills. Being the reigning Olympic champion in decathlon is of limited value in off years. People admire the medal but don't have much use for you otherwise. It's like they want you to go away and reappear just in time for the next Games.

Sarah and I found ourselves in the midst of a legitimate financial crisis. I had a mortgage due in two weeks and no money coming in. If I competed again before fully recovering, I might hurt myself and have to retire early. Should I look at other jobs and give up training altogether? Certainly supporting my family was more important than the pursuit of a third medal.

All the stress I had felt leading up to 2008 seemed to return with a vengeance. I felt the pain of losing income, just as anyone does when laid off from a job. I went through stages of grief and loss. And the next week I was scheduled to compete in a decathlon: the USA vs. Germany meet.

> Certainly supporting my family was more important than the pursuit of a third medal.

I packed up my troubles and headed to San Diego for the competition, but I performed terribly. My knee was still hurting, so I pulled out, knowing I could hurt it worse and perhaps end my career if

I forced it. I immediately had knee surgery, and the doctors removed a benign growth. I began to patch up but still had no income. All my medals looked lovely but didn't seem to help us now.

"God, what do I do?" I prayed deep into the night, unable to sleep. "Should I get a job coaching somewhere? Will I have to retire? What about all the dreams I had? What about my goals for 2012?"

Recovering from surgery forced me to pull out of world championships, but that was the least of my concerns. My faith was being stretched beyond any limit I had known by the situation with our finances.

Sarah and I were living on savings and began preparing to change our living situation, perhaps moving in with our parents or to a lower-cost state. I woke up every morning, wondering how I would provide food for my family. Sarah and I grew closer, and while we did not argue, at times the kids could tell we were stressed out.

I began to feel bitter. I was a decorated decathlete, a veteran in the sport, owner of two Olympic medals, and winner of unprecedented back-to-back indoor world championships with enough other medals to fill a vault. I had achieved the second highest score in USA decathlon history and the third highest in heptathlon. Yet it seemed no one was there to give me a pat on the back or an "attaboy," much less a sponsorship. It was like I had stepped out of the limelight of Beijing and become invisible.

Strength to Keep Going

"Why am I doing this?" I asked Kevin one day. "Why try to win a third medal, if this is the reward? What's the point? And how long can I really be the best? Other guys are starting to catch up with me. I think God is telling me I need to be done. This situation is His way of telling me to quit."

Kevin shook his head slowly. "I just don't see that, Bryan. There's more for you. I just believe it."

Many people around me were saying the same thing. Over the next few weeks I received calls and texts from friends saying, "Bryan, we're praying for you, and we feel this is not the time for you to quit. There is more for you in the sport. Keep going."

Though it was tempting to hang up my cleats, I listened to those voices and obeyed what I felt God telling me. In a time of prayer one day, I laid it all out for Him: "You're in control," I prayed. "There's nothing I can do right now to change this situation. I don't have a sponsor. I'm not competing. But we're still in our house. We haven't really lost anything. I'm going to have an attitude of trust that this will all work out, the same way You've worked things out in the past."

Within days sponsor interest began to pour in as if released by some heavenly floodgate. BMW signed a deal with me and leased a car to me. The Century Council, which lobbies against underage drinking, made me one of its spokesmen. BP, the oil and gas company, got behind me with an amazing deal that included a big donation to my foundation and a monthly gas stipend.

> Though it was tempting to hang up my cleats, I listened to those voices and obeyed what I felt God telling me.

God not only was providing but also meeting my basic needs for transportation and groceries, as if to say, "And you thought I wasn't listening."

There were other sponsors: Visa, Straub Hospital, and more. By the time my agent, Jeremy, was finished, it was the best year I'd had in terms of sponsorships. I had gained so much more than I had lost.

That financial peace released new energy into my mind and body. I trained like never before. Peace, focus, and newfound joy made competition fun. God had met my family's needs, and I felt good again.

Another Chance

I am eagerly anticipating the 2012 Olympics, but it feels different this time—and better.

I am one of the veterans. The up-and-comers are eight or nine years younger than I am, and I'm something of a mentor to them, if you measure mentorship by the number of texts we send to each other. I have spent some time training with guys such as Trey Hardee and getting to know Ashton a lot better.

Many of the names associated with the sport when I first began to be noticed are no longer competing at the highest level—Roman, Tomas, Tom Pappas, Dmitri Karpov. Some still compete but mostly for the love of the sport. I feel blessed to have gone up against those decathlon greats and others such as Erki Nool and Jon-Arnar Magnusson. They taught me about the event, the proud history, how to train, how to compete, how to lose, and how to win. They are the elders of the decathlon, and I think of them every time I step onto the track. I am carrying the legacy of the sport they passed on to me.

My goal now is to do the best I can and leave my own lasting mark on the sport. I want to break the world record. And I want to become the first decathlete to medal for a third time. That's what the 2012 Olympics is about for me.

At the time of this writing, these goals are still ahead of me. Making the U.S. team in 2012 will be harder than ever, and that's good. It means the

> I am eagerly anticipating the 2012 Olympics, but it feels different this time—and better.

decathlon is strong in the U.S. right now. Trey and Ashton have scored 8,700. I have a best score of 8,800 and feel better than ever. It should be an awesome thing to watch us compete for those precious few slots.

More than ever I compete for the joy of serving God. Every ounce of energy I pour onto the track is a form of worship. The fear of losing has gone away. I compete hard so I can honor Him and obey His plan and build a bigger platform for the benefit of my family and the kids who will be blessed through my foundation.

No matter what happens, I have already won. God has provided for us every step of the way, my doubts aside. He has made my dreams come true. Instead of competing afraid, as I did sometimes when I was younger, I compete with faith, freedom, and a sense of high privilege. I am at the peak of my abilities, physically and mentally, and I see the results every day on the track.

I'm back. And I am ready to win.

EPILOGUE

God loves the story of an unlikely champion, and that is the story He has told through my life. Along the way He has given me "stones of remembrance," a phrase I borrow from the story of Joshua leading the nation of Israel into the promised land. As the Israelites crossed over that day, God instructed them to take with them stones from the river to remind them of His faithfulness. When their children asked what the stones meant, they told the story of what God had done for them.

My gold medal, my silver medal, every victory I have had on the athletic field—each one is a stone of remembrance for me, for my children, and, I hope, for many others.

They remind me of God's faithfulness. That faithfulness extends to everyone. I feel that I have been put on earth not only to win medals and enjoy the thrill of competition but also, ultimately, to point people to the faithfulness of God. When they ask for proof, I point to my life and my past.

I point to the people who God put in my life at key times along the way.

I point to the critical decisions that brought me closer to Him.

I point to the principles He taught me along the way.

I point to all of these stones of remembrance.

> I feel that I have been put on earth not only to win medals and enjoy the thrill of competition but also, ultimately, to point people to the faithfulness of God.

All of the credit goes to God. And I am happy to give it.

Let me ask you before I end this book: What are your stones of remembrance? Has God given you a great family? Success in business? A particular skill? He has been good to every one of us. What can you point to when people ask about your life? How do you tell them about God's faithfulness?

It is not a matter of being perfect. I think of my mom, raising us alone for a while, overcoming the regret of divorce and rebuilding her life. She wasn't perfect, but you do not have to be perfect for God to work in your situation. My mom gave her best in offering prayers and in loving my brother and me when few other people did. Some days the best she had was to get us ready for school and herself ready for work. That was all she had. Other days she had much more. I know that I am still reaping the benefits of what my mom did back then, and I will continue reaping them for the rest of my life. I believe her prayers for me reverberate through heaven even now.

And there is more to come for me.

The Bryan Clay Foundation, which I started in 2005, is my response to God's faithfulness and my effort to tell other people, especially children, about it. My heart is especially tender toward young kids who have experienced fatherlessness. I speak to groups of kids in many settings to tell them what God has done in my life and how they, too, can follow Him. I want them to know that I share their feelings and their experiences, and I found the Father who matters most. I want them to gain strength from my story and my example. I want them to see that when they put God first, life can be far better than they imagine.

I want to give them hope.

I am still living by the principles that God has taught me along the way, and I continue to learn new ones all the time. They help me to live and compete for His glory. On this journey I am learning who I really am, who God made me to be, what I am able to do, and how hard I can push myself. I like that challenge.

All of the credit goes to God. And I am happy to give it.

It can be your challenge too. I hope you will grab hold of God's faithfulness and start gathering stones of remembrance for yourself and those who will follow. That is the enduring legacy that will far outlast the headlines, the victories of life, and even the highest achievements we can reach.

Ultimately what matters is what we do for God's glory. Those things will grow brighter with age until one day they shine like the sun.

ACKNOWLEDGMENTS

I want to thank every person in my life who has been with me on this journey and proved to be a valuable friend, family member, or mentor. There are too many to name, but I appreciate each of you more than you know. Whatever success God has given me humbles me and would not have happened without your influence in my life. Thank you.